Psychosis and Schizophrenia:
Thinking It Through

Every effort has been made in preparing this book to provide accurate and up-to-date information that is in accord with accepted standards and practice at the time of publication. Nevertheless, the author, editors, and publisher can make no warranties that the information contained herein is totally free from error, not least because clinical standards are constantly changing through research and regulation. The author, editors, and publisher therefore disclaim all liability for direct or consequential damages resulting from the use of material contained in this book. Readers are strongly advised to pay careful attention to information provided by the manufacturer of any drugs or equipment that they plan to use.

PUBLISHED BY NEI PRESS, an imprint of NEUROSCIENCE EDUCATION INSTITUTE
Carlsbad, California, United States of America

NEUROSCIENCE EDUCATION INSTITUTE
1930 Palomar Point Way, Suite 101
Carlsbad, California 92008

http://www.neiglobal.com

Printed in the United States of America
First Edition, August 2010

Typeset in Myriad Pro

Library of Congress Cataloging-in-Publication Data
ISBN 1-4225-0012-9

Table of Contents

CME Information

Overview
The aim of this booklet is to explain the underlying pathophysiology of schizophrenia and psychosis and describe how currently available and novel antipsychotic agents may work to ameliorate symptoms and bring about side effects. Chapter 1 discusses the neurobiology believed to underlie the positive, negative, cognitive, and affective symptoms of schizophrenia. Chapter 2 describes the mechanisms by which antipsychotic agents may reduce symptoms while bringing about adverse effects. Chapter 3 outlines currently available antipsychotic agents and discusses novel agents that may one day be available. Chapter 4 presents suggestions for ways to optimize functional outcomes in patients being treated for schizophrenia.

Target Audience
This activity has been developed for prescribers specializing in psychiatry. There are no prerequisites for this activity. Health care providers in all specialties who are interested in psychopharmacology, especially primary care physicians, nurses, psychologists, and pharmacists, are welcome for advanced study.

Statement of Need
The following unmet needs regarding psychosis and schizophrenia were revealed following a critical analysis of activity feedback, literature review and through new medical knowledge:

- Schizophrenia is a debilitating disorder associated with poor quality of life, low remission rates, and huge adherence issues.
- Cognitive impairment is severe and pervasive in the schizophrenia population and tends to be independent of other clinical symptoms, yet is not currently a diagnostic requirement.
- Several new medications are soon to be introduced and research into additional new treatment methods is ongoing; clinicians need to be educated on these new treatment strategies as data accumulate so that they are prepared to implement these tools once they become available.

To help fill these unmet needs, quality improvement efforts need to:

- Provide education regarding cognitive impairment in schizophrenia, including current research on its biology and pharmacology, proposals for its inclusion in DSM-V, and clinical guidance on how it should be measured and differentiated from negative symptoms
- Provide education regarding optimization of treatment strategies for schizophrenia, including consideration of minimizing side effects and maximizing adherence
- Provide education regarding new treatment strategies for schizophrenia, including novel mechanisms of action, and how these new options can help fill unmet needs within the current treatment of schizophrenia

Learning Objectives
After completing this activity, participants should be better able to:

- Understand the importance of cognitive factors in schizophrenia, including evolving new diagnostic criteria and methods for assessing cognition in clinical practice
- Differentiate antipsychotic drug treatments from each other on the basis of pharmacologic mechanisms and evidence-based clinical trial results
- Develop treatment strategies that are designed to enhance adherence
- Combine practical experience with evolving new evidence in order to integrate new and soon-to-be introduced treatments into clinical practice

Accreditation and Credit Designation Statements
The Neuroscience Education Institute is accredited by the Accreditation Council for Continuing Medical Education to provide continuing medical education for physicians.

The Neuroscience Education Institute designates this educational activity for a maximum of 3.0 *AMA PRA Category 1 Credits* ™. Physicians should only claim credit commensurate with the extent of their participation in the activity.

Also available will be a certificate of participation for completing this activity.

Nurses in most states may claim full credit for activities approved for *AMA PRA Category 1 Credits*™ (for up to half of their recertification credit requirements). This activity is designated for 3.0 AMA PRA Category 1 Credits.

Activity Instructions

This CME activity is in the form of a printed monograph and incorporates instructional design to enhance your retention of the information and pharmacological concepts that are being presented. You are advised to go through the figures in this activity from beginning to end, followed by the text, and then complete the posttest and activity evaluation. The estimated time for completion of this activity is 3.0 hours.

Instructions for CME Credit

To receive your certificate of CME credit or participation, please complete the posttest (you must score at least 70% to receive credit) and activity evaluation found at the end of the monograph and mail or fax them to the address/number provided. Once received, your posttest will be graded and a certificate sent if a score of 70% or more was attained. Alternatively, **you may complete the posttest and activity evaluation online and immediately print your certificate.** There is no fee for CME credits for this activity.

NEI Disclosure Policy

It is the policy of the Neuroscience Education Institute to ensure balance, independence, objectivity, and scientific rigor in all its educational activities. Therefore, all individuals in a position to influence or control content development are required by NEI to disclose any financial relationships or apparent conflicts of interest that may have a direct bearing on the subject matter of the activity. Although potential conflicts of interest are identified and resolved prior to the activity being presented, it remains for the participant to determine whether outside interests reflect a possible bias in either the exposition or the conclusions presented.

These materials have been peer-reviewed to ensure the scientific accuracy and medical relevance of information presented and its independence from commercial bias. The Neuroscience Education Institute takes responsibility for the content, quality, and scientific integrity of this CME activity.

Individual Disclosure Statements
Author
Debbi Ann Morrissette, PhD
Medical Writer, Neuroscience Education Institute, Carlsbad, CA
No other financial relationships to disclose.

Content Editors
Meghan Grady
Director, Content Development, Neuroscience Education Institute, Carlsbad, CA
No other financial relationships to disclose.

Stephen M. Stahl, MD, PhD
Adjunct Professor, Department of Psychiatry, University of California, San Diego School of Medicine
Honorary Visiting Senior Fellow, University of Cambridge, UK
Grant/Research: AstraZeneca; Boehringer Ingelheim; Bristol-Myers Squibb; Cephalon; Dainippon Sumitomo; Forest; Lilly; Lundbeck; Novartis; Pamlab; Pfizer; Pfizer Canada; Pharmasquire; sanofi-aventis; Schering-Plough; Shire; Wyeth
Consultant/Advisor: Allergan; AstraZeneca; BioMarin; Biovail; Boehringer Ingelheim; Bristol-Myers Squibb; CeNeRx; Covance; Cypress; Dainippon Sumitomo; Eisai; Forest; GlaxoSmith Kline; Labopharm; Lilly; Lundbeck; Marinus; MEDACorp/Leerink Swann; Meiji; Merck; Novartis; Pamlab; Pfizer; Pfizer Canada; Pierre Fabre; Prexa; Propagate; Royalty; sanofi-aventis; Schering-Plough; Shire; SK; Sofinnova; Solvay; Vanda; Wyeth
Speakers Bureau: Pfizer; Schering-Plough; Wyeth

Peer Reviewer
Steven S. Simring, MD, MPH
Director of Forensic Training, Department of Psychiatry, Columbia University College of Physicians and Surgeons, New York State Psychiatric Institute, New York City
No other financial relationships to disclose.

Design Staff
Nancy Muntner
Director, Medical Illustrations, Neuroscience Education Institute, Carlsbad, CA
No other financial relationships to disclose.

Program Development
The following are employed by Neuroscience Education Institute in Carlsbad, CA, and have no other financial relationships to disclose.
Rory Daley, MPH, *Associate Director, Program Development*
Steve Smith, *President and COO*

Disclosed financial relationships have been reviewed by the Neuroscience Education Institute CME Advisory Board to resolve any potential conflicts of interest. All faculty and planning committee members have attested that their financial relationships do not affect their ability to present well-balanced, evidence-based content for this activity.

Disclosure of Off-Label Use
This educational activity may include discussion of products or devices that are not currently labeled for such use by the FDA. Please consult the product prescribing information for full disclosure of labeled uses.

Disclaimer
The information presented in this educational activity is not meant to define a standard of care, nor is it intended to dictate an exclusive course of patient management. Any procedures, medications, or other courses of diagnosis or treatment discussed or suggested in this educational activity should not be used by clinicians without full evaluation of their patients' conditions and possible contraindications or dangers in use, review of any applicable manufacturer's product information, and comparison with recommendations of other authorities. Primary references and full prescribing information should be consulted.

Participants have an implied responsibility to use the newly acquired information from this activity to enhance patient outcomes and their own professional development. The participant should use his/her clinical judgment, knowledge, experience, and diagnostic decision-making before applying any information.

Sponsorship Information
This activity is sponsored by Neuroscience Education Institute.

 Neuroscience Education Institute

Support
This activity is supported by an educational grant from Sepracor / Dainippon Sumitomo Pharma.

Date of Release/Expiration
Release Date: August 1, 2010   CME Credit Expiration Date: July 31, 2013

1

Neurobiology of Schizophrenia

Chapter 1 aims to describe the hypothetical neurobiology of schizophrenia thought to underlie the symptoms of the disorder. The dopamine hypothesis of schizophrenia has been accepted for a long time, especially as the first antipsychotics were shown to block dopamine D2 receptors. In addition, theories about the involvement of glutamate and serotonin have gained momentum in the pathophysiology of schizophrenia. This chapter will show that schizophrenia does not necessarily result from a hypo- or hyperactive dopamine system, but that it might be more accurate to say that dopamine is "out of tune." Additionally, this chapter will give a brief overview of how dopamine, serotonin, and glutamate neurotransmitter systems may converge to induce the positive (e.g. hallucinations), negative (e.g. depression), cognitive, and affective symptoms of schizophrenia.

Key Dopamine Pathways

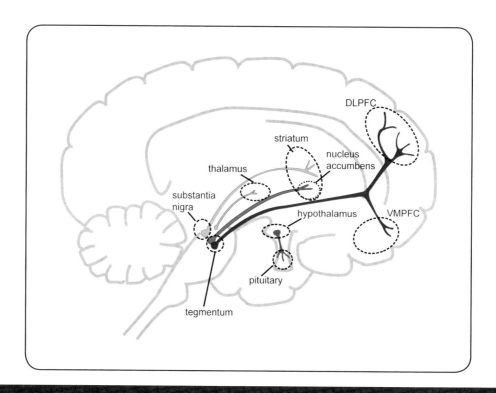

FIGURE 1.1. Five dopamine (DA) pathways are relevant in explaining the symptoms of schizophrenia and the therapeutic and side effects of antipsychotic drugs. The nigrostriatal DA pathway is part of the extrapyramidal nervous system, which controls motor function and movement. The mesolimbic DA pathway is part of the brain's limbic system, which regulates behaviors, including pleasurable sensations, the powerful euphoria of drugs of abuse, and the delusions and hallucinations seen in psychosis. The mesocortical DA pathway is implicated in mediating the cognitive symptoms (dorsolateral prefrontal cortex, DLPFC), affective symptoms (ventromedial prefrontal cortex, VMPFC), and negative symptoms of schizophrenia. The tuberoinfundibular DA pathway projects from the hypothalamus to the anterior pituitary gland and controls prolactin secretion. The fifth DA pathway arises from multiple sites, including the periaqueductal gray, ventral mesencephalon, hypothalamic nuclei, and lateral parabrachial nucleus, and projects to the thalamus. Its function is not well known.

The Dopamine Hypothesis of Schizophrenia:
Positive Symptoms

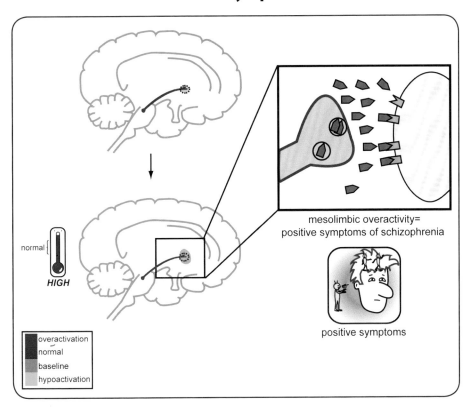

mesolimbic overactivity=
positive symptoms of schizophrenia

positive symptoms

FIGURE 1.2. The mesolimbic dopamine (DA) pathway, which sends DA projections from cell bodies in the ventral tegmental area to the nucleus accumbens in the ventral striatum, is the main candidate thought to regulate the positive symptoms of psychosis. Specifically, it has been hypothesized that hyperactivity of this pathway accounts for the delusions and hallucinations observed in schizophrenia. This hypothesis is known both as the "DA hypothesis of schizophrenia" and perhaps more precisely as the "mesolimbic DA hyperactivity hypothesis of positive symptoms of schizophrenia".

The Dopamine Hypothesis of Schizophrenia: Negative, Cognitive, and Affective Symptoms

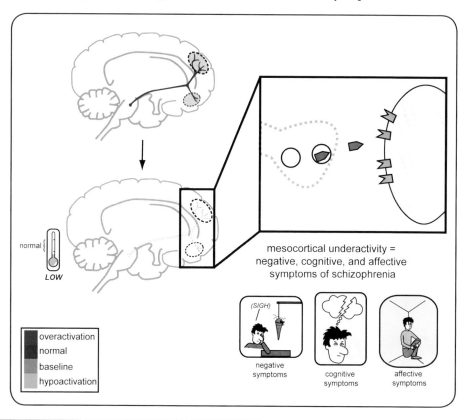

FIGURE 1.3. The mesocortical dopamine (DA) pathway is hypothetically also affected in schizophrenia. Here, DA cell bodies in the ventral tegmental area send projections to the DLPFC to regulate cognition and executive functions and to the VMPFC to regulate emotions and affect. Hypoactivation of this pathway theoretically results in the negative, cognitive, and affective symptoms seen in schizophrenia. This hypothesis is sometimes called the "mesocortical DA hypoactivity hypothesis of negative, cognitive, and affective symptoms" of schizophrenia. This DA deficit could result from ongoing degeneration due to glutamate excitotoxicity or from a neurodevelopmental impairment in the glutamatergic system. The loss of motivation and interest, anhedonia, and lack of pleasure observed in schizophrenia result not only from a deficient mesocortical DA pathway, but also from a malfunctioning mesolimbic DA pathway.

The Integrated Dopamine Hypothesis of Schizophrenia

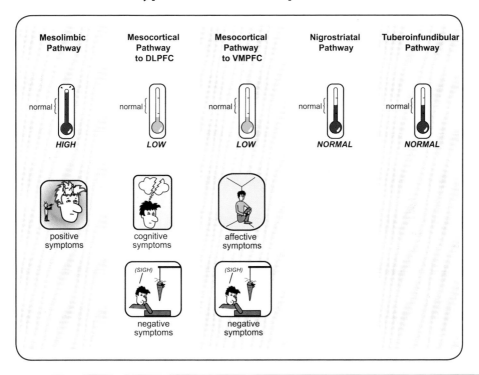

FIGURE 1.4. In schizophrenia, it appears that some dopamine (DA) pathways are overactive (mesolimbic pathway), others are underactive (mesocortical pathway), and others function normally (nigrostriatal and tuberoinfundibular pathway). Thus, the DA system is neither "all too high" nor "all too low," but rather "out of tune," and DA needs to be increased in some areas, decreased in others, and left untouched in other sets of circuits. Various antipsychotic drugs acting at different receptor subtypes, especially blocking D2 receptors and serotonin 2A (5HT2A) receptors, seek to put the system back "in tune." Alternatively, regulating DA output by modulating transmitters such as glutamate may prove to be another way to "normalize" or "tune" DA circuits.

Key Glutamate Pathways

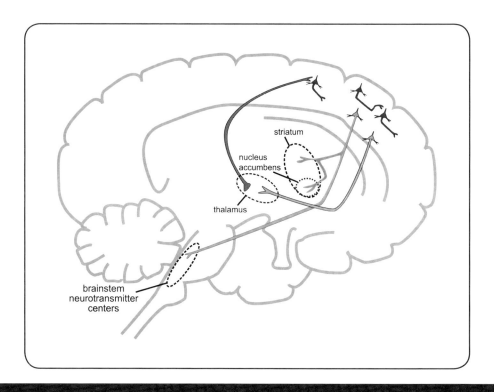

FIGURE 1.5. There are five glutamate pathways in the brain that are of particular relevance to schizophrenia. The cortical brainstem glutamate projection descends from layer 5 pyramidal neurons in the prefrontal cortex to brainstem neurotransmitter centers, including the raphe (serotonin), the locus coeruleus (norepinephrine), and the ventral tegmental area and substantia nigra (DA). This projection mainly regulates neurotransmitter release in the brainstem. The cortico-striatal glutamate pathway descends from the prefrontal cortex to the striatum, and the cortico-accumbens glutamate pathway sends projections to the nucleus accumbens. These pathways make up the "cortico-striatal" portion of cortico-striatal-thalamic loops. Thalamo-cortical glutamate pathways encompass pathways ascending from the thalamus and innervating pyramidal neurons in the cortex. Cortico-thalamic glutamate pathways descend from the PFC to the thalamus. The cortico-cortical glutamatergic pathways allow intracortical pyramidal neurons to communicate with each other.

NMDA Receptor Hypofunction
Hypothesis of Schizophrenia

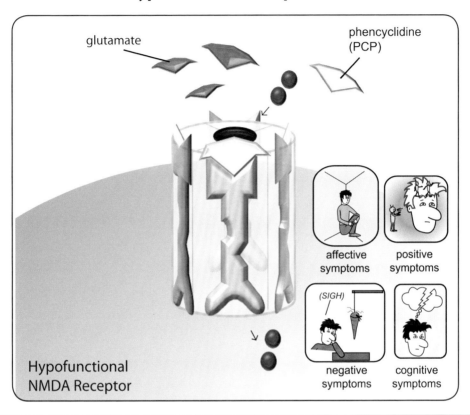

FIGURE 1.6. The NMDA (N-methyl-d-aspartate) receptor hypofunction hypothesis has been put forth in an attempt to explain mesolimbic dopamine (DA) hyperactivity. This hypothesis relies on the observation that when normal humans ingest phencyclidine (PCP), an NMDA receptor antagonist, they experience positive symptoms very similar to those observed in schizophrenia, such as hallucinations and delusions. Thus, hypoactive glutamate NMDA receptors could theoretically explain the biological basis for the mesolimbic DA hyperactivity. PCP also induces affective symptoms such as blunted affect, negative symptoms such as social withdrawal, and cognitive symptoms such as executive dysfunction in normal humans. Hypofunctional NMDA receptors might therefore be involved in all symptoms of schizophrenia.

Role of Glutamate in Schizophrenia

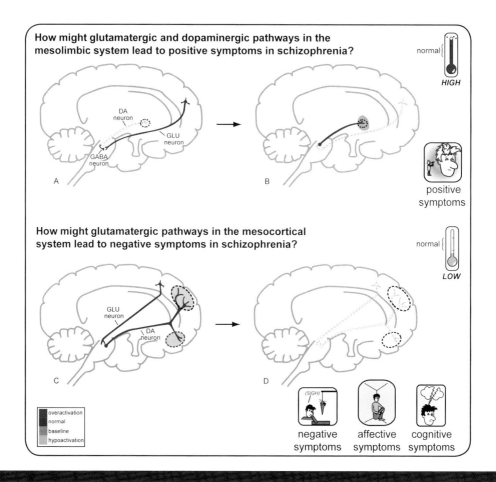

FIGURE 1.7. (A) The descending cortico-brainstem glutamate pathway normally leads to tonic inhibition of the mesolimbic dopamine (DA) pathway via gamma-aminobutyric acid (GABA) interneurons in the ventral tegmental area. (B) When glutamate projections become hypoactive, this tonic inhibition is hypothetically missing, leading to hyperactivity of the mesolimbic DA pathway, which could explain the overactivity of the mesolimbic DA pathway in schizophrenia. (C) In the ventral tegmental area, the cortico-brainstem glutamate projections can also directly synapse onto DA neurons, thus tonically exciting the mesocortical DA pathway. (D) Hypoactivity in glutamate projections (similar to what is observed following phencyclidine administration) can thus theoretically result in lost activation of the mesocortical DA neurons and might be the cause of the negative, cognitive, and affective symptoms seen in schizophrenia.

Opposing Actions of 5HT1A and 5HT2A Receptors on Dopamine Release

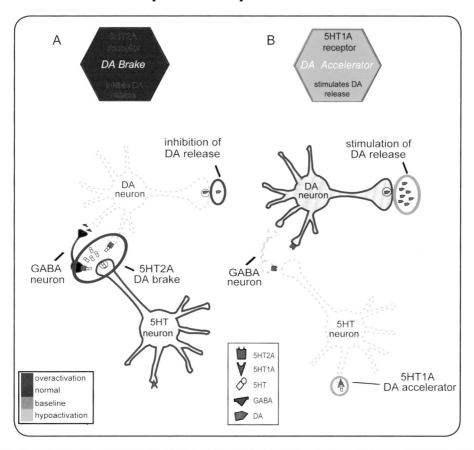

FIGURE 1.8. Serotonin (5HT) can regulate DA release directly or indirectly and can have various effects on dopamine (DA) neurons. Specifically, 5HT1A and 5HT2A receptors have opposite actions on DA release. (A) Stimulation of 5HT2A receptors inhibits DA release; thus, 5HT2A receptors act as a DA brake. When 5HT binds to 5HT2A receptors on DA neurons or on GABA neurons, DA release is decreased directly or via inhibition through GABA release, respectively. (B) Stimulation of 5HT1A receptors increases DA release, and thus 5HT1A receptors act as a DA accelerator. Upon binding to 5HT1A receptors, 5HT causes inhibition of its own release. A lack of 5HT results in disinhibition of DA release and therefore increased DA output.

Regulation of Dopamine Release by Serotonin in the Nigrostriatal Pathway

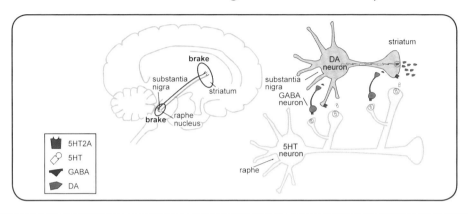

FIGURE 1.9. In the nigrostriatal pathway, the serotonin (5HT)-dopamine (DA) interaction mediates extrapyramidal side effects. Here, 5HT can regulate DA release by acting on the somatodendritic regions of the DA neuron in the substantia nigra or by acting on the axonal regions of the DA neuron in the striatum. In the absence of 5HT, DA is freely released in the striatum.

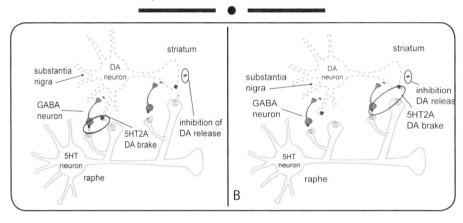

FIGURE 1.10. (A) When 5HT is released from raphe projections to the substantia nigra (red circle on the left), it stimulates postsynaptic somatodendritic 5HT2A receptors on DA and GABA neurons. This will lead to inhibition of axonal DA release (red circle on the right). (B) When serotonin (5HT) is released from a synaptic connection projecting from axoaxonal contacts or by volume neurotransmission between 5HT and dopamine (DA) axon terminals (red circle, bottom), it will stimulate postsynaptic 5HT2A receptors on DA and GABA neurons, leading to decreased axonal DA release (red circle, top).

Somatodendritic Blockade of 5HT2A Receptors Leads to Increased Dopamine Release

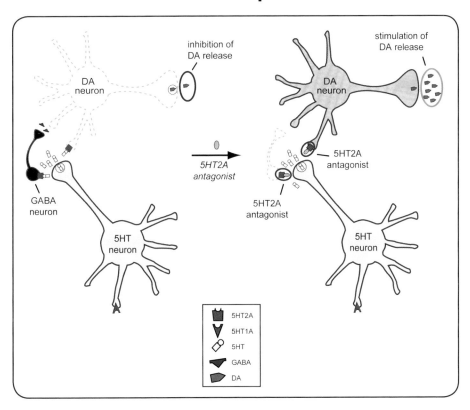

FIGURE 1.11. If stimulation of 5HT2A receptors leads to decreased dopamine (DA) release, then blocking 5HT2A receptors via antagonists should result in increased DA release. Increasing DA release can therefore be obtained by either blocking 5HT2A receptors on postsynaptic DA neurons or by blocking 5HT2A receptors on GABA interneurons.

Serotonin Also Modulates Cortical Glutamate Release

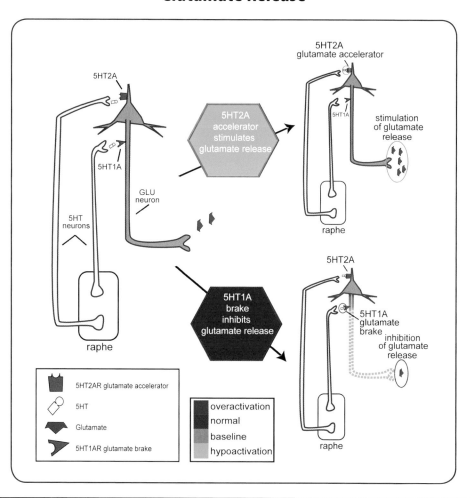

FIGURE 1.12. Stimulation of 5HT2A and 5HT1A receptors also leads to an opposing modulation of cortical glutamate release, but does so contrary to the actions of these same serotonin (5HT) receptors upon dopamine (DA) release. Here, stimulation of 5HT2A receptors located on glutamate cell bodies induces an increase in glutamate release, acting as a glutamate accelerator. Stimulation of 5HT1A receptors located on glutamate axons inhibits glutamate release, acting as a glutamate brake. This is contrary to the regulation that 5HT has on DA release (see Figure1.8), whereby stimulation of 5HT2A receptors leads to inhibition of DA release (brake) and stimulation of 5HT1A receptors leads to increased DA release (accelerator).

2

Pharmacology and Side Effects of Antipsychotics

Chapter 2 aims to explain the complex pharmacology of antipsychotics and recognize how different antipsychotic drugs affect the various symptoms of schizophrenia. Additionally, this chapter aims to elucidate how side effects are linked to the drug's receptor profile.

The serendipitous discovery in the 1950s that the antihistamine chlorpromazine can relieve symptoms of psychosis led to the discovery of conventional antipsychotics. Their ability to block D2 receptors was recognized by the 1970s. Since then, much research has been done to improve antipsychotic medications. This chapter explores the different classes of antipsychotics, elaborating on their properties and describing the most common side effects associated with antipsychotics.

Conventional Antipsychotics

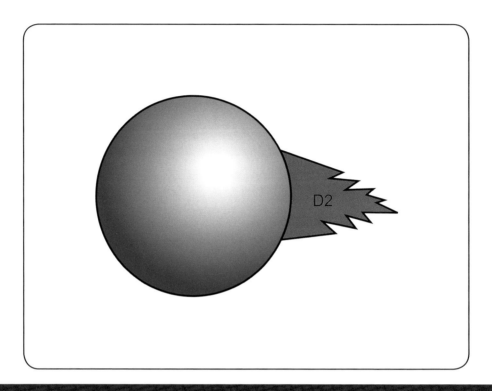

FIGURE 2.1. Conventional antipsychotics treat the symptoms of schizophrenia by blocking D2 receptors. Excessive blockade of D2 receptors or blockade of DA receptors in hypoactive areas can lead to many side effects, including "neurolepsis," an extreme form of slowness or absence of motor movement (nigrostriatal pathway); increased prolactin (tuberoinfundibular pathway); and the worsening of negative, cognitive, and affective symptoms (mesocortical pathways).

Side Effects Due to Chronic D2 Blockade

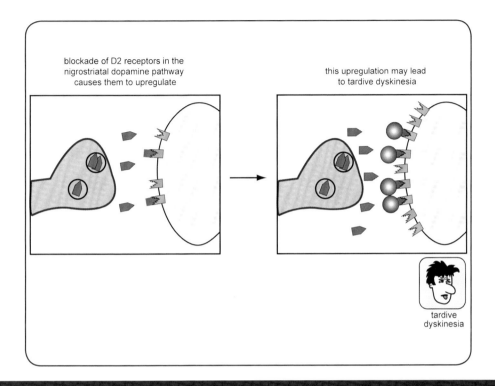

blockade of D2 receptors in the
nigrostriatal dopamine pathway
causes them to upregulate

this upregulation may lead
to tardive dyskinesia

tardive
dyskinesia

FIGURE 2.2. Long-term blockade of D2 receptors in the nigrostriatal DA pathway can lead to tardive dyskinesia, a hyperkinetic movement disorder characterized by facial and tongue movements (e.g., tongue protrusions, facial grimaces, chewing) as well as quick, jerky limb movements. Chronic administration of conventional antipsychotics can lead to D2 receptor supersensitivity, or upregulation, whereby an increase in receptor number attempts to overcome the drug-induced receptor blockade.

Every year, 5% of patients on conventional antipsychotics will develop tardive dyskinesia (25% of patients will be affected by 5 years), and for a disorder that starts in the early 20s, these odds are unacceptable.

Removing the conventional antipsychotic in time can prevent the occurrence of tardive dyskinesia, as this will allow the D2 receptors to lose their sensitivity and downregulate. However, if this is not done in time, irreversible molecular changes take place, leading to tardive dyskinesia. Patients developing EPS early in their treatment appear to be more susceptible to tardive dyskinesia and need to be monitored closely.

Additional Side Effects of Conventional Antipsychotics

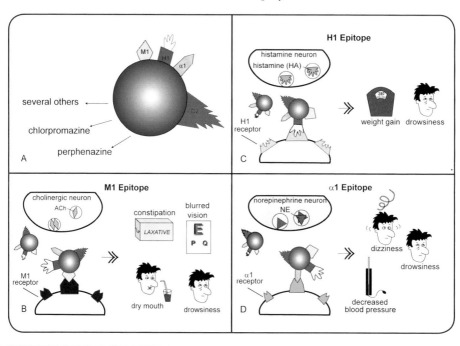

FIGURE 2.3. (A) Besides blockade at D2 receptors, conventional antipsychotics have additional pharmacologic properties: blockade of M1 muscarinic cholinergic receptors, H1 histamine receptors, and alpha1 adrenergic receptors. Medications with this receptor profile will exhibit similar side effects. (B) The M1 muscarinic anticholinergic portion of the drug can lead to constipation, blurred vision, dry mouth, and drowsiness when bound to acetylcholine receptors. (C) The H1 histamine portion of the drug can lead to drowsiness and weight gain. (D) The alpha 1 adrenergic portion of the drug can lead to dizziness, decreased blood pressure, and drowsiness.

Properties of Atypical Antipsychotics

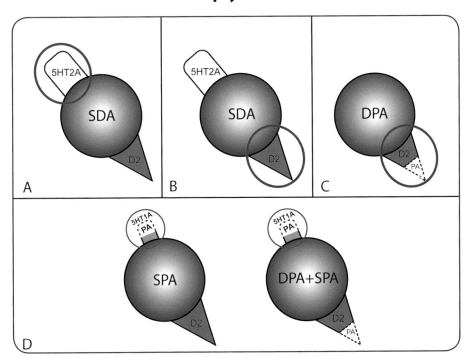

FIGURE 2.4. Atypical antipsychotics represent the second generation of antipsy-chotics. They are distinguished from conventional antipsychotics by their clinical properties (low extrapyramidal side effects and good efficacy for negative symp-toms), as well as by four pharmacological characteristics: (A) Atypical antipsychot-ics couple their D2 antagonism with 5HT2A antagonism (SDA). (B) The dissociation rate at the D2 receptor sets apart the "atypicality" of an antipsychotic. Tight and long-lasting binding is characteristic of conventional antipsychotics, whereas rapid dissociation is a feature of atypical antipsychotics. (C) Atypical antipsychotics can also be D2 partial agonists (DPAs). These agents bind in a manner that is nei-ther too antagonizing nor too stimulating, allowing for just the "right" amount of neurotransmission at D2 receptors. (D) Full or partial agonism at the 5HT1A recep-tor (SPA) can also be a characteristic of some atypical antipsychotics. Stimulation at the 5HT1A receptor can increase dopamine release, thus improving affective, cognitive, and negative symptoms while reducing the risk of extrapyramidal side effects and prolactin elevation. Serotonin1A agonism can also decrease glutamate release, which may indirectly reduce the positive symptoms of psychosis.

Pharmacological Profile of Atypical Antipsychotics

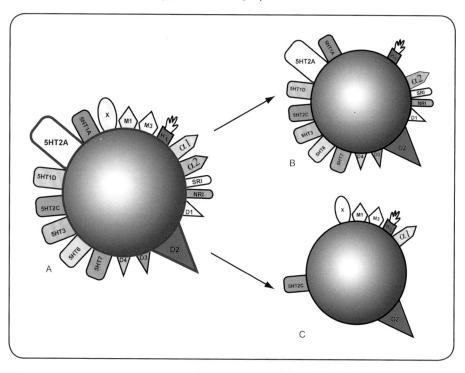

FIGURE 2.5. One characteristic of atypical antispychotics is their vast pharmacological profile. (A) In addition to being D2 and 5HT2A blockers, they interact with more receptors of the DA and 5HT family, such as 5HT1A, 5HT1D, 5HT2C, 5HT3, 5HT6, and 5HT7 receptors; the 5HT transporter; and D1, D3, and D4 receptors. They also interact with receptors of other neurotransmitters, such as the norepinephrine transporter and the muscarinic 1 and 3, histamine 1, and alpha 1 and 2 adrenergic receptors. The "X" functional group represents the unclear actions that some atypical antipsychotics have on the insulin system, where they change cellular insulin resistance and increase fasting plasma triglyceride levels. (B) Whereas some of the different pharmacological properties of atypical antipsychotics contribute to their therapeutic effects, (C) others can actually elicit side effects. No two atypical antipsychotics have identical binding properties, which probably helps to explain how they all have somewhat distinctive clinical properties.

Combined 5HT2A/D2 Receptor
Blockade Leads to Less EPS

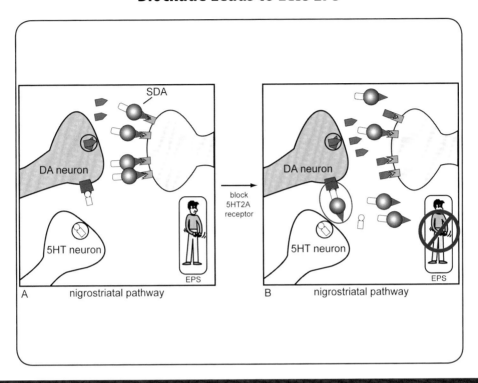

FIGURE 2.6. (A) When postsynaptic D2 receptors are blocked by antagonists, especially in the long-term, this can result in the occurrence of EPS. This can also occur with 5HT2A/D2 antagonists if only the DA blocking property is active.

(B) When both D2 and 5HT2A receptors are blocked by SDAs, then the 5HT2A blockade actually opposes the actions of the D2 blockade. Blocking 5HT2A receptors leads to increased DA release, as 5HT normally inhibits DA release. Increased levels of DA in the synapse will then compete with SDAs for the D2 receptors on the postsynaptic neurons, thus preventing full inhibition. Reversal of D2 blockade therefore prevents the occurrence of EPS, similar to what is seen in compounds with rapid D2 dissociation.

Effects of 5HT2A Blockade in the Mesocortical DA Pathway

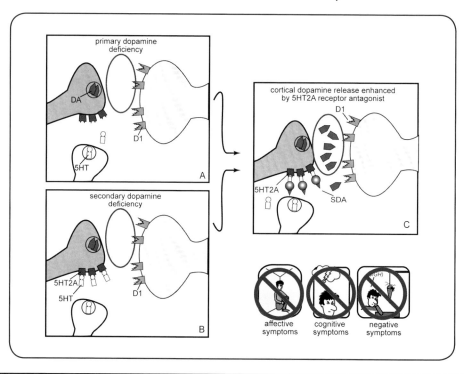

FIGURE 2.7. Affective, cognitive, and negative symptoms are thought to be the result of a lack of DA stimulation in the mesocortical pathway. DA deficiency could be (A) primary or (B) secondary due to excess release of 5HT (5HT inhibits DA release).

(C) Blockade of 5HT2A receptors following administration of SDAs should actually lead to increased synaptic DA levels, which could compensate for the DA deficiency and relieve affective, cognitive, and negative symptoms. It is possible that amelioration of affective, cognitive, and negative symptoms may contribute to improvement in functional outcomes compared to reduction solely in positive symptoms with D2 antagonists or partial agonists.

Prolactin Regulation by DA and
5HT in the Tuberoinfundibular Pathway

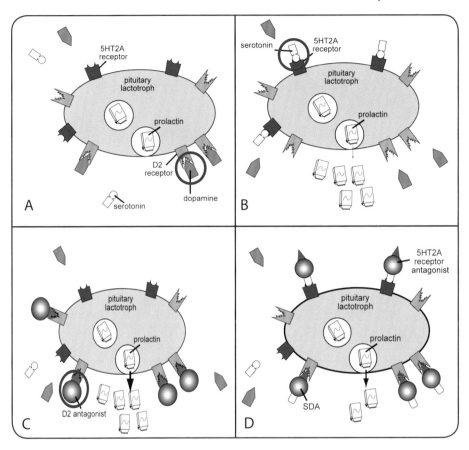

FIGURE 2.8. (A) Under normal conditions, DA is inhibitory to prolactin release from pituitary lactotroph cells by binding to D2 receptors in the pituitary gland. (B) When 5HT binds to 5HT2A receptors on pituitary lactotroph cells, prolactin release is increased. Thus, 5HT and DA regulate prolactin release in an opposing manner. (C) Due to their antagonism at D2 receptors, conventional antipsychotics block the inhibitory action that DA has on prolactin and therefore lead to increased prolactin release. (D) Atypical antipsychotics such as 5HT2A/D2 antagonists allow normal levels of prolactin to be secreted. Whereas blocking D2 receptors increases prolactin release, blocking 5HT2A receptors blocks the D2-induced release of prolactin. Thus, antagonism at one receptor subtype cancels the action of blocking the other receptor, and no net change is observed in prolactin release.

Rapid Dissociation Theory of Atypical Antipsychotic Action

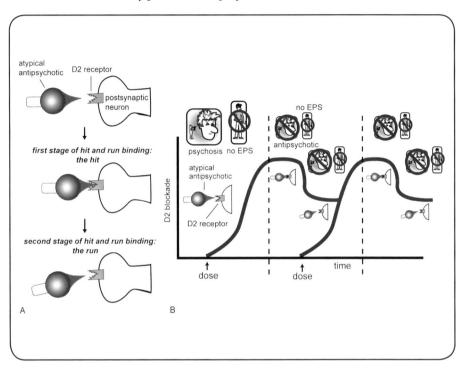

FIGURE 2.9. (A) Unlike conventional antipsychotics, atypical antipsychotics do not have "teeth" on their binding site, meaning that they cannot be locked into position upon binding to D2 receptors. Atypical antipsychotics interact loosely with D2 receptors, exemplified by their smooth binding site. This results in a rapid dissociation from the binding site, also referred to as the "hit and run" receptor binding property. Thus, during the "hit," the atypical antipsychotic does not get locked into the receptor binding site and is able to "run" and slip away easily.

(B) An untreated patient with schizophrenia exhibits positive symptoms but no extrapyramidal side effects (EPS). Upon administration of an atypical antipsychotic, the D2 receptors get blocked for only a short period of time, in contrast to the long-lasting blockade from conventional antipsychotics. Only short blockade of D2 receptors is theoretically required for antipsychotic action, whereas persistent blockade of D2 receptors is required for EPS to occur. Atypical antipsychotics are beneficial in treating the positive symptoms of schizophrenia while preventing EPS, as dose after dose they bind just long enough to D2 receptors to induce antipsychotic effects, but they "run away" before eliciting EPS.

Conventional vs. Atypical Antipsychotics

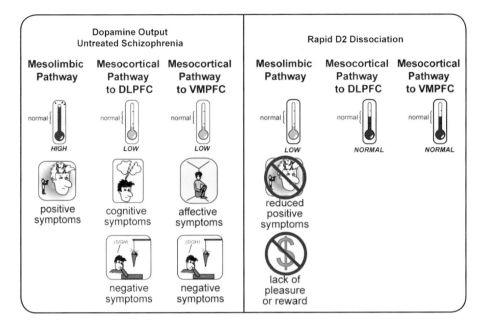

FIGURE 2.10. A D2 antagonist reduces dopamine (DA) output indiscriminately throughout the brain. While positive symptoms of psychosis will be successfully reduced, the experience of pleasure, which is also mediated by the mesolimbic DA pathway, will be impaired. Decreasing DA output in the hypoactive mesocortical DA pathways will further reduce this pathway's activity and can actually worsen cognitive, negative, or affective symptoms. By reducing dopamine (DA) output in the nigrostriatal DA pathway, D2 antagonists can lead to extrapyramidal side effects (EPS) and tardive dyskinesia. Chronic blockade of the tuberoinfundibular DA pathway will result in hyperprolactinemia and its accompanying complications.

Conventional vs. Atypical Antipsychotics

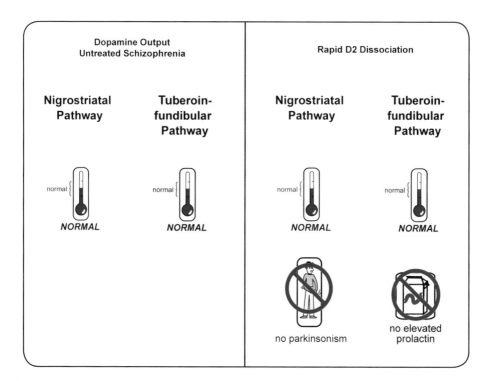

FIGURE 2.11. Administration of an agent that rapidly dissociates from D2 receptors leads to a reduced DA output in the mesolimbic DA pathway, thus decreasing positive symptoms. Unfortunately, decreasing DA output in this pathway can also lower the experiences of pleasure and reward. Loose binding of atypical antipsychotics in the mesocortical DA pathway could potentially reset this pathway. Theoretically, persistent blockade of D2 receptors is needed in this pathway to worsen affective, cognitive, or negative symptoms. Thus, rapid blockade of and dissociation from D2 receptors in the mesocortical DA pathway may not lead to these side effects. In the nigrostriatal and tuberoinfundibular DA pathways, administration of agents that rapidly dissociate from D2 receptors may exhibit reduced risk of EPS and may not lead to elevated prolactin levels, thus preventing some of the unwanted side effects inherent in conventional antipsychotics.

The Agonist Spectrum:
The Theory Behind Partial Agonists

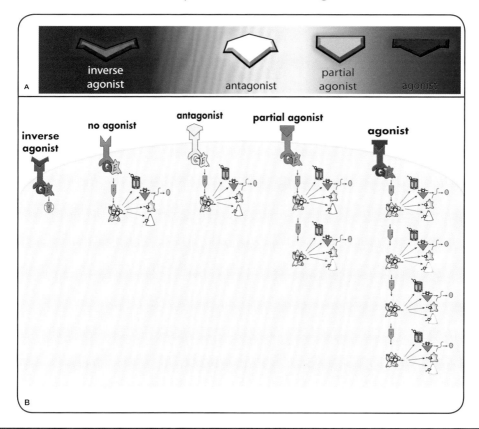

FIGURE 2.12. (A) Naturally occurring neurotransmitters, as well as drugs that stimulate receptors, are primary agonists. Drugs that stimulate a receptor to a lesser degree are partial agonists or stabilizers. Antagonists are "silent" and only block the action of agonists without having an action of their own. Inverse agonists can block the actions of the agonist, or they can reduce baseline activity in the absence of an agonist. (B) The concept of the agonist spectrum can also be adapted to the signal transduction system. A full agonist leads to maximal signal transduction; a partial agonist leads to a level of signal transduction between the full agonist and no agonist. Antagonists can only reduce the level of signal transduction caused by the agonist. Inverse agonists, on the other hand, can actually lead to lower levels of stimulation beyond what is normally produced in the absence of an agonist.

How is the Dopamine Spectrum Related to Receptor Output?

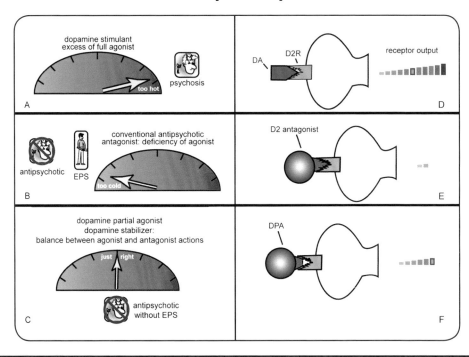

FIGURE 2.13. (Left) In order to understand the actions of dopamine (DA) and DA agents within an agonist spectrum, it may be helpful to look at them along a "hot-cold" spectrum. (A) DA acts as the ultimate agonist and is too "hot," resulting in psychosis. (B) D2 blockers such as conventional antagonists are too "cold," and while they prevent psychotic episodes, they also lead to extrapyramidal side effects (EPS). (C) Partial agonists are "lukewarm," leading to just the right stimulation of DA receptors, thus preventing psychotic episodes without inducing EPS. (Right) In terms of output, (D) DA is the ultimate full agonist, leading to full receptor output. (E) At the other end of the spectrum, conventional antipsychotics (full antagonists) lead to very little DA output. The atypical antipsychotics that have 5HT2A/D2 blocking activity also lead to little DA output. (F) D2 partial agonists (DPAs), on the other hand, stimulate DA receptors only partially, leading to an intermediate or moderate output.

D2 and D3 Partial Agonists: Overview

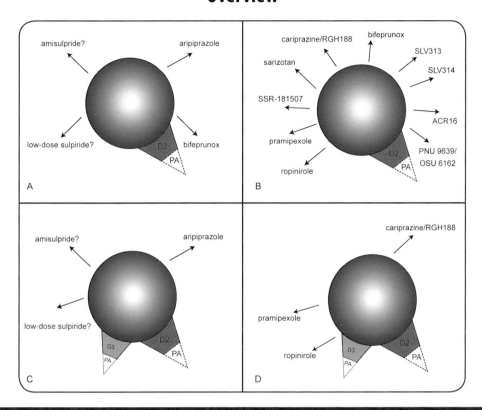

FIGURE 2.14. (A) There is currently only one well-established dopamine (DA) partial agonist on the market: aripiprazole. Bifeprunox is a D2 partial agonist, but it was recently not approved by the FDA. Amisulpride and sulpiride are available outside the US and may act as partial agonists, particularly at low doses, but are not well characterized as DA partial agonists. (B) DA partial agonists currently in development include cariprazine/RGH188, bifeprunox, SLV313, SLV314, ACR16, SSR181507, and sarizotan. These agents are closer to the antagonist end of the partial agonist spectrum. D2 partial agonists that are closer to the full agonist end of the spectrum include pramipexole and ropinirole. These agents are in testing for bipolar depression and treatment-resistant depression, but they are not yet approved for these uses. (C and D) Often not emphasized in their pharmacological characterization is the fact that most atypical antipsychotics act at D3 receptors, mostly as antagonists. Aripiprazole, however, acts as a D3 partial agonist. Amisulpride and sulpiride could also be D3 partial agonists. It is not clear what this action adds to D2 partial agonist action, but there is no selective D2 partial agonist nor any selective D3 partial agonist currently available.

5HT1A Partial Agonism of Atypical Antipsychotics

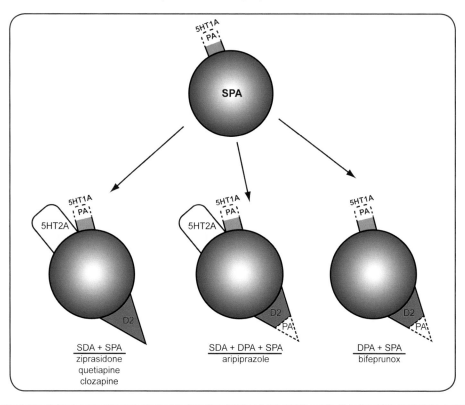

FIGURE 2.15. Various antipsychotics do not fit neatly into a single class of drugs because they combine different receptor actions. In addition to being 5HT2A/D2 blockers, ziprasidone, quetiapine, and clozapine are partial agonists at 5HT1A receptors. The D2 partial agonist aripiprazole is also an antagonist at 5HT2A receptors and a partial agonist at 5HT1A receptors. Besides being a D2 partial agonist, bifeprunox is a partial agonist at the 5HT1A receptor. This molecular polypharmacy is what makes these compounds different from each other and explains their different effectiveness in various individuals with specific ailments.

Which Receptors Can Hypothetically Lead to Cardiometabolic Risk or Sedation?

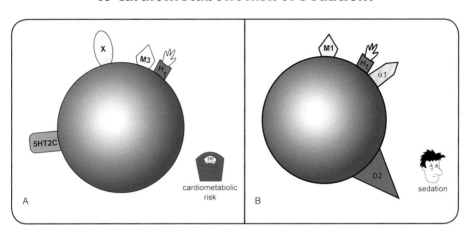

FIGURE 2.16. (A) There are a few functional groups that may hypothetically increase cardiometabolic risk; these include 5HT2C, muscarinic M3, and histamine H1 receptors as well as receptors yet to be identified (signified here as "X"). Specifically, 5HT2C and H1 antagonism is linked to weight gain, and M3 receptor antagonism can alter insulin regulation. Functional group "X" may increase insulin resistance, resulting in elevated fasting plasma triglyceride levels. Some patients might be more likely than others to experience increased cardiometabolic risk on certain atypical antipsychotics. Simultaneous blockade of 5HT2C and H1 receptors can lead to weight gain, which might result from increased appetite stimulation via hypothalamic eating centers. (B) D2, M1, H1, and alpha1 adrenergic receptor antagonism can all lead to sedation. Thus, the atypical antipsychotics with those receptor properties will at some level or another alter arousal in patients. Acetylcholine (ACh), histamine (HA), and norepinephrine (NE) are all involved in arousal pathways, thereby connecting neurotransmitter centers with the thalamus, hypothalamus, basal forebrain, and cortex. Thus, it is predictable that atypical antipsychotics with pharmacologic actions that block these receptors could be associated with sedative effects.

Metabolism of Antipsychotics by CYP450 Enzymes

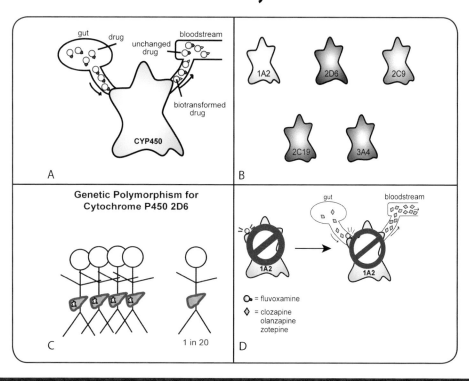

FIGURE 2.17. (A) The cytochrome P450 (CYP450) enzyme system, which is located in the gut wall and liver, is responsible for the way the body metabolizes drugs such as antipsychotics. When the drug substrate passes through the gut, it is biotransformed into a product and released into the bloodstream. Thus, upon administration, a drug is partially metabolized by the CYP450 system and partially left unchanged. (B) The CYP450 system encompasses a large number of enzymes; the five most common and relevant systems are CYP450 1A2, 2D6, 2C9, 2C19, and 3A4. (C) An individual's genetic makeup determines which CYP450 enzymes s/he has. For example 1 in 20 Caucasians is a poor metabolizer via 2D6 and thus needs to metabolize drugs by an alternate route. This may (1) not be as metabolically efficient and (2) explain the different efficacy of various antipsychotics in different patients. (D) Different drug classes are substrates for different CTP450 enzymes. For example, the antipsychotics clozapine, olanzapine, and zotepine are substrates for CYP450 1A2. If these are given in combination with an antidepressant such as fluvoxamine, which acts as an inhibitor of this enzyme, plasma levels can rise. Thus, it is important to know which drugs a patient is taking and to be prepared for the need to adjust dosages.

3

Currently Available Antipsychotics and Upcoming Antipsychotics With Novel Mechanisms of Action

Chapter 3 aims to describe individual antipsychotic medications that are currently available. Dosing tips, side effect profiles, and drug interactions are provided in addition to currently understood receptor binding properties for each antipsychotic. In general, none of the currently available antipsychotics (conventional or atypical) work well enough to allow patients to fulfill personal goals or function in society. This shortcoming may be due to inadequate treatment of the negative and/or cognitive symptoms that are also associated with schizophrenia. This chapter introduces several new medications that are being studied for their unique receptor profiles and novel mechanisms of action. These may someday be more successful in improving functional outcomes for those with schizophrenia.

Symbols Used in this Chapter			
	Life-threatening or Dangerous Side Effects		Drug Interactions
	Tips and Pearls		Cardiac Impairment
	Children and Adolescents		Renal Impairment
	Pregnancy		Hepatic Impairment

Aripiprazole

Aripiprazole is the first atypical antipsychotic with D2 partial agonist properties. Its 5HT2A and 5HT1A features may be the reason for its increased tolerability and efficacy. Aripiprazole is effective in treating positive and manic symptoms, and it may be useful for depression. Its benefits also lie in its many different formulations (tablets, disintegrating tablets, liquid, and IM formulations). Aripiprazole is usually devoid of sedative side effects, and can even be activating. For some patients, aripiprazole is either too close to a full antagonist or too close to a full agonist. In both cases, dose adjustment and the timing of administration can ameliorate these symptoms. Similar to ziprasidone, aripiprazole causes little to no weight gain, most likely because it lacks 5HT2C and histamine H1 properties. Additionally, aripiprazole does not seem to induce dyslipidemia, increase fasting triglyceride levels, or increase insulin resistance. Thus, aripiprazole has a lower cardiometabolic risk.

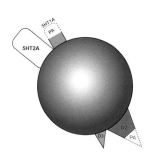

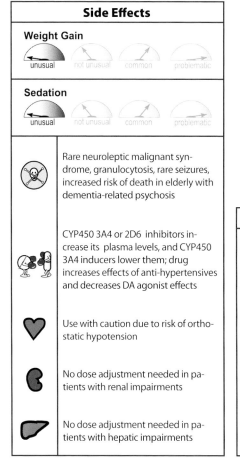

Side Effects

Weight Gain

unusual | not unusual | common | problematic

Sedation

unusual | not unusual | common | problematic

Rare neuroleptic malignant syndrome, granulocytosis, rare seizures, increased risk of death in elderly with dementia-related psychosis

CYP450 3A4 or 2D6 inhibitors increase its plasma levels, and CYP450 3A4 inducers lower them; drug increases effects of anti-hypertensives and decreases DA agonist effects

Use with caution due to risk of orthostatic hypotension

No dose adjustment needed in patients with renal impairments

No dose adjustment needed in patients with hepatic impairments

Pearls

May be activating; no diabetes or dyslipidemia risk; favorable tolerability profile; for some, less may be more; for others, more may be more; may be useful in bipolar depression

Approved for schizophrenia (age 13 to 17), bipolar (age 10 to 17), and irritability in autistic children (age 6 to 17)

Pregnancy risk category C (some animal studies show adverse effects; no controlled studies in humans)

Asenapine

Asenapine is one of the newer atypical antipsychotics with 5HT2A/D2 antagonist properties. Antagonist actions at 5HT2C receptors and alpha 2 receptors suggest potential antidepressant properties. Because asenapine is not absorbed after swallowing (<2% bioavailable orally), it must be administered sublingually, which increases the bioavailability to 35%. A common side effect is hypoesthesia, and patients may not eat or drink for 10 minutes after sublingual administration to avoid the drug being washed into the stomach, where it will not be absorbed. Sublingual administration may require prescribing asenapine to reliable and compliant patients or those who have someone who can supervise drug administration.

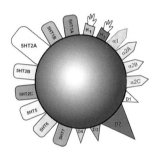

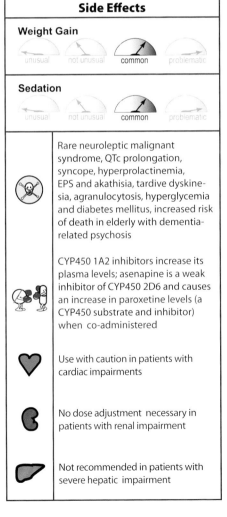

Side Effects			
Weight Gain			
unusual	not unusual	common	problematic
Sedation			
unusual	not unusual	common	problematic

Rare neuroleptic malignant syndrome, QTc prolongation, syncope, hyperprolactinemia, EPS and akathisia, tardive dyskinesia, agranulocytosis, hyperglycemia and diabetes mellitus, increased risk of death in elderly with dementia-related psychosis

CYP450 1A2 inhibitors increase its plasma levels; asenapine is a weak inhibitor of CYP450 2D6 and causes an increase in paroxetine levels (a CYP450 substrate and inhibitor) when co-administered

Use with caution in patients with cardiac impairments

No dose adjustment necessary in patients with renal impairment

Not recommended in patients with severe hepatic impairment

Pearls	
	Tablets dissolve in saliva under tongue within seconds and should not be swallowed; drinking and eating should be avoided for 10 minutes after administration.
	Efficacy and safety not established in children and adolescents
	Pregnancy risk category C (some animal studies show adverse effects; no controlled studies in humans); recommended to stop breastfeeding

Clozapine

Clozapine is considered the "prototypical" atypical antipsychotic and leads to few EPS, does not result in tardive dyskinesia and does not elevate prolactin levels. It has proven particularly efficacious when other antipsychotics fail. Even though it is very effective, clozapine is not considered a first-line agent because it can lead to the potentially life-threatening side effect agranulocytosis. Weight increase and the concomitant risk of developing metabolic complications are greatest with clozapine.

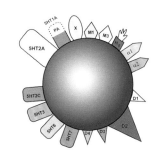

Side Effects

Weight Gain

unusual   not unusual   common   problematic

Sedation

unusual   not unusual   common   problematic

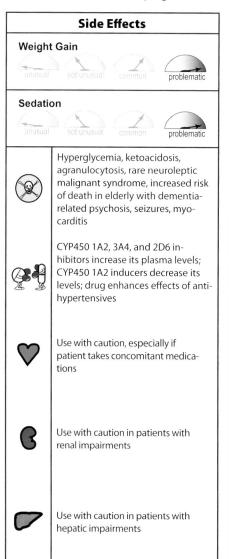

Hyperglycemia, ketoacidosis, agranulocytosis, rare neuroleptic malignant syndrome, increased risk of death in elderly with dementia-related psychosis, seizures, myo-carditis

CYP450 1A2, 3A4, and 2D6 in-hibitors increase its plasma levels; CYP450 1A2 inducers decrease its levels; drug enhances effects of anti-hypertensives

Use with caution, especially if patient takes concomitant medica-tions

Use with caution in patients with renal impairments

Use with caution in patients with hepatic impairments

Pearls

Rapid discontinuation can lead to rebound psychosis; most efficacious but most dangerous; reduces suicide in schizophrenia

Potentially efficacious in early-onset, treatment-resistant schizophrenia; children and adolescents should be monitored more often than adults

Pregnancy risk category B (animal studies do not show adverse effects; no controlled studies in humans)

Iloperidone

Iloperidone is one of the newer atypical antipsychotics with 5HT2A/D2 antagonistic properties. In patients developing orthostasis or when adding to or switching from another drug with alpha 1 antagonist properties, it may be necessary to titrate very slowly. Patients most sensitive to orthostasis include the young, the elderly, those with cardiovascular problems, and those with concomitant vasoactive drugs. The 18 to 33 hour half-life also theoretically supports once daily dosing as a possibility.

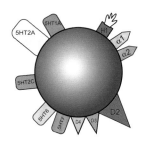

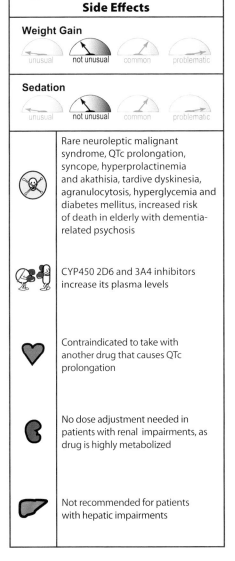

Side Effects

Weight Gain

unusual — **not unusual** — common — problematic

Sedation

unusual — **not unusual** — common — problematic

Rare neuroleptic malignant syndrome, QTc prolongation, syncope, hyperprolactinemia and akathisia, tardive dyskinesia, agranulocytosis, hyperglycemia and diabetes mellitus, increased risk of death in elderly with dementia-related psychosis

CYP450 2D6 and 3A4 inhibitors increase its plasma levels

Contraindicated to take with another drug that causes QTc prolongation

No dose adjustment needed in patients with renal impairments, as drug is highly metabolized

Not recommended for patients with hepatic impairments

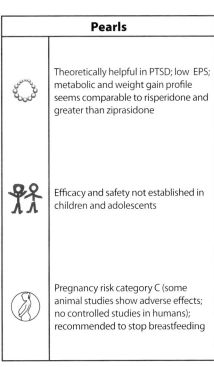

Pearls

Theoretically helpful in PTSD; low EPS; metabolic and weight gain profile seems comparable to risperidone and greater than ziprasidone

Efficacy and safety not established in children and adolescents

Pregnancy risk category C (some animal studies show adverse effects; no controlled studies in humans); recommended to stop breastfeeding

Olanzapine

Olanzapine is a 5HT2A/D2 antagonist whose chemical structure is very similar to that of clozapine. Even at high doses, olanzapine only induces mild EPS, emphasizing its atypical nature. Although olanzapine has M1, H1, and alpha 1 antagonistic properties, it is not as sedating as clozapine. It is one of the antipsychotics with the greatest cardiometabolic risk, as it leads to weight gain, increased fasting triglyceride levels, and increased insulin resistance. Olanzapine often exhibits better efficacy and effectiveness at higher doses. Olanzapine appears to be effective at reducing affective and cognitive symptoms, a property most likely related in part to its 5HT2C antagonism. Olanzapine comes in different formulations, including oral disintegrating tablets and intramuscular formulations.

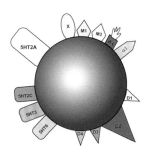

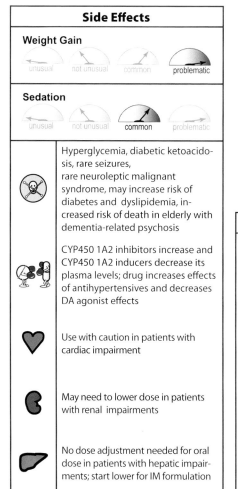

Side Effects

Weight Gain

unusual / not unusual / common / **problematic**

Sedation

unusual / not unusual / **common** / problematic

☠	Hyperglycemia, diabetic ketoacidosis, rare seizures, rare neuroleptic malignant syndrome, may increase risk of diabetes and dyslipidemia, increased risk of death in elderly with dementia-related psychosis
(drug interaction icon)	CYP450 1A2 inhibitors increase and CYP450 1A2 inducers decrease its plasma levels; drug increases effects of antihypertensives and decreases DA agonist effects
♥	Use with caution in patients with cardiac impairment
(kidney icon)	May need to lower dose in patients with renal impairments
(liver icon)	No dose adjustment needed for oral dose in patients with hepatic impairments; start lower for IM formulation

Pearls

(pills icon)	More may be more; doses above 15 mg/day are useful for acutely ill/agitated patients; IM formulation can be given to initiate oral dosing; rapid onset without titration
(adolescents icon)	Recently approved for adolescents aged 13 to 17
(pregnancy icon)	Pregnancy risk category C (some animal studies show adverse effects; no controlled studies in humans)

Paliperidone

Paliperidone, also a 5HT2A/D2 antagonist, is the active metabolite of risperidone, and thus has a similar receptor profile. The oral sustained-release formulation of paliperidone allows it to be taken just once a day. In some patients, this property could lead to less EPS and sedation compared to its parent compound. It might however be associated with weight gain, insulin resistance, and diabetes as well as prolactin elevation, similarly to risperidone. Paliperidone is the first atypical antipsychotic that has recently been approved as a once-monthly formulation for the acute and maintenance treatment of schizophrenia in the United States.

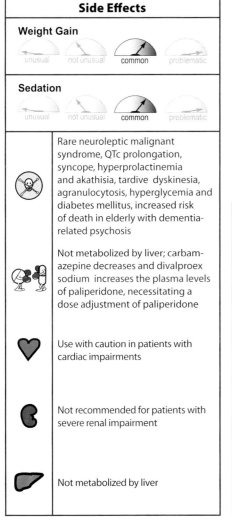

Side Effects

Weight Gain

unusual · not unusual · common · problematic

Sedation

unusual · not unusual · common · problematic

Rare neuroleptic malignant syndrome, QTc prolongation, syncope, hyperprolactinemia and akathisia, tardive dyskinesia, agranulocytosis, hyperglycemia and diabetes mellitus, increased risk of death in elderly with dementia-related psychosis

Not metabolized by liver; carbamazepine decreases and divalproex sodium increases the plasma levels of paliperidone, necessitating a dose adjustment of paliperidone

Use with caution in patients with cardiac impairments

Not recommended for patients with severe renal impairment

Not metabolized by liver

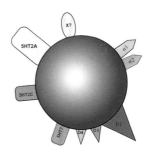

Pearls

Dose-dependent risk of EPS; may elevate prolactin levels and cause weight gain (especially at higher doses); once-monthly formulation

Preliminary study suggests efficacy in children and adolescents; however, safety in patients younger than age 18 has not been established

Not recommended during pregnancy or breastfeeding; insufficient data in humans

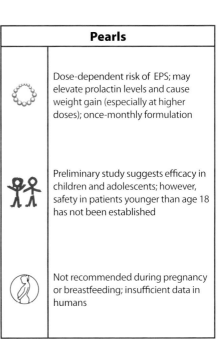

Quetiapine

The 5HT2A/D2 antagonist quetiapine is chemically related to clozapine. Its active metabolite, norquetiapine, has unique features that most likely add to quetiapine's efficacy. This very atypical antipsychotic exhibits rapid D2 dissociation and therefore hardly any EPS and no prolactin elevation. The partial 5HT1A agonist feature of quetiapine and the norepinephrine reuptake-inhibiting and 5HT2C-blocking properties of norquetiapine are most likely responsible for its effectiveness at treating mood and cognitive disorders. Quetiapine is effective as a once-daily dose, and if given in the evening, it will not induce daytime sedation.

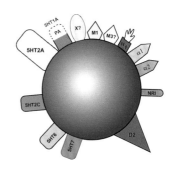

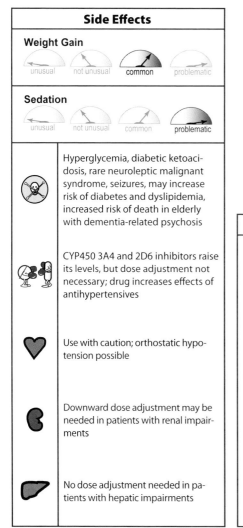

Side Effects	
Weight Gain	unusual — not unusual — **common** — problematic
Sedation	unusual — not unusual — common — **problematic**

	Hyperglycemia, diabetic ketoacidosis, rare neuroleptic malignant syndrome, seizures, may increase risk of diabetes and dyslipidemia, increased risk of death in elderly with dementia-related psychosis
	CYP450 3A4 and 2D6 inhibitors raise its levels, but dose adjustment not necessary; drug increases effects of antihypertensives
	Use with caution; orthostatic hypotension possible
	Downward dose adjustment may be needed in patients with renal impairments
	No dose adjustment needed in patients with hepatic impairments

Pearls	
	Is often underdosed, but even low doses can be sedating; moderate to high doses are associated with metabolic side effects; no motor side effects; no prolactin elevation; also available in an extended release formulation
	Recently approved for children and adolescents (age 10 to 17 for acute manic episodes in bipolar disorder, age 13 to 17 for schizophrenia)
	Pregnancy risk category C (some animal studies show adverse effects; no controlled studies in humans)

Risperidone

Risperidone is mostly a 5HT2A/D2 antagonist. At low doses, risperidone behaves like an atypical antipsychotic, but if the doses are pushed, it can, like conventional drugs, lead to EPS. Risperidone is also available as an intramuscular, long-term depot formulation that lasts two weeks. Risperidone does increase prolactin levels, but there appears to be less risk of weight gain and cardiometabolic risk with it than with some other atypical antipsychotics, at least in some patients.

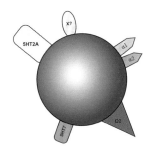

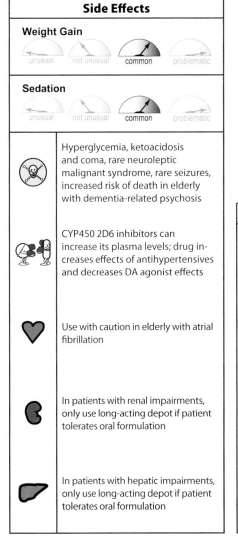

Side Effects	
Weight Gain	
unusual / not unusual / **common** / problematic	
Sedation	
unusual / not unusual / **common** / problematic	
☠	Hyperglycemia, ketoacidosis and coma, rare neuroleptic malignant syndrome, rare seizures, increased risk of death in elderly with dementia-related psychosis
	CYP450 2D6 inhibitors can increase its plasma levels; drug increases effects of antihypertensives and decreases DA agonist effects
♥	Use with caution in elderly with atrial fibrillation
	In patients with renal impairments, only use long-acting depot if patient tolerates oral formulation
	In patients with hepatic impairments, only use long-acting depot if patient tolerates oral formulation

Pearls	
	Less may be more; good treatment for agitation (elderly) and behavioral symptoms (children); dose-dependent EPS
	Approved for autism-related irritability (ages 5 to 16), bipolar (ages 10 to 17), schizophrenia (ages 13 to 17)
	Pregnancy risk category C (some animal studies show adverse effects; no controlled studies in humans)

Ziprasidone

Ziprasidone is a chemically different compound with interesting pharmacology. Due to its 5HT2A/D2 blocking capability, it reduces the risk of EPS and elevated prolactin levels. Ziprasidone has been shown to treat both positive and negative symptoms. In cases of acute psychosis, the intramuscular formulation is highly effective. Rapid dose escalation to middle to high doses has been proven to be most effective. Ziprasidone does not induce weight gain, dyslipidemia, elevation of fasting triglycerides, or insulin resistance. The 5HT1D antagonist actions combined with the 5HT and NE reuptake-blocking properties might contribute to the absence of weight gain induction by ziprasidone.

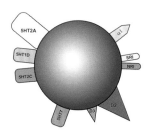

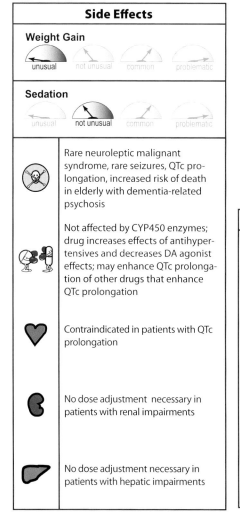

Side Effects

Weight Gain

unusual · not unusual · common · problematic

Sedation

unusual · not unusual · common · problematic

☠	Rare neuroleptic malignant syndrome, rare seizures, QTc prolongation, increased risk of death in elderly with dementia-related psychosis
💊	Not affected by CYP450 enzymes; drug increases effects of antihypertensives and decreases DA agonist effects; may enhance QTc prolongation of other drugs that enhance QTc prolongation
♥	Contraindicated in patients with QTc prolongation
🫘	No dose adjustment necessary in patients with renal impairments
🫀	No dose adjustment necessary in patients with hepatic impairments

Pearls

📿	It is often underdosed; activation occurs at 20–40 mg 2X/day and is reduced at 60–80 mg 2X/day; food doubles bioavailability
👫	Recently approved for children and adolescents with mania (age 10 to 17)
🤰	Pregnancy risk category C (some animal studies show adverse effects; no controlled studies in humans)

Sertindole

Sertindole is an atypical antipsychotic with 5HT2A/D2 antagonist properties. Despite having the potential for QTc prolongation, sertindole is being carefully introduced into clinical practice in some countries along with careful dosing and EKG monitoring guidelines because some patients who do not benefit from other antipsychotics may benefit from it. EKGs should be repeated when steady state is reached, at 3 weeks after treatment initiation, then every 3 months during treatment, prior to and after any dose increase, after the addition of any drug that can affect the concentration of sertindole, and upon reaching a dose of 16 mg. This medication is currently in Phase IV clinical trials and may be available in the United States in the future.

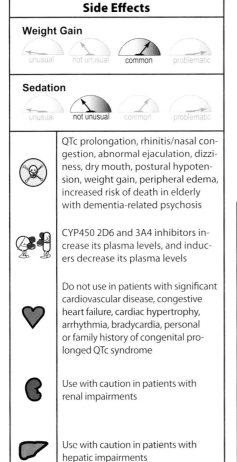

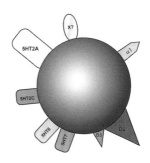

Side Effects

Weight Gain

unusual — not unusual — **common** — problematic

Sedation

unusual — **not unusual** — common — problematic

QTc prolongation, rhinitis/nasal congestion, abnormal ejaculation, dizziness, dry mouth, postural hypotension, weight gain, peripheral edema, increased risk of death in elderly with dementia-related psychosis

CYP450 2D6 and 3A4 inhibitors increase its plasma levels, and inducers decrease its plasma levels

Do not use in patients with significant cardiovascular disease, congestive heart failure, cardiac hypertrophy, arrhythmia, bradycardia, personal or family history of congenital prolonged QTc syndrome

Use with caution in patients with renal impairments

Use with caution in patients with hepatic impairments

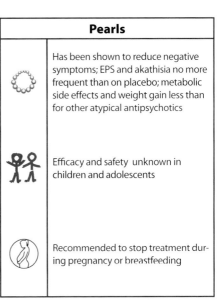

Pearls

Has been shown to reduce negative symptoms; EPS and akathisia no more frequent than on placebo; metabolic side effects and weight gain less than for other atypical antipsychotics

Efficacy and safety unknown in children and adolescents

Recommended to stop treatment during pregnancy or breastfeeding

Cariprazine

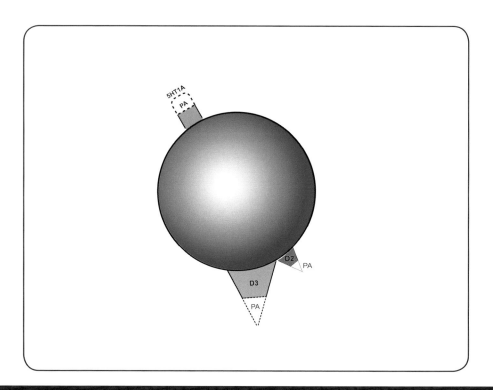

FIGURE 3.1. Cariprazine is a dopamine partial agonist currently in clinical testing. It is the only agent with stronger affinity for D3 over D2 receptors, with both actions being partial agonist actions rather than antagonist actions. This compound is in testing for schizophrenia, acute bipolar mania, bipolar depression, and treatment-resistant depression, and has provided some preliminary evidence of clinical efficacy in acute schizophrenia and mania. Cariprazine seems to be more of an agonist than the related partial agonist aripiprazole, but less of an agonist within the agonist spectrum than bifeprunox. Dosing, efficacy, and side effects are still under investigation, but little weight gain or metabolic problems have been identified thus far. Cariprazine has two long-lasting active metabolites with potential for development as a weekly, biweekly, or even monthly oral depot.

Lurasidone

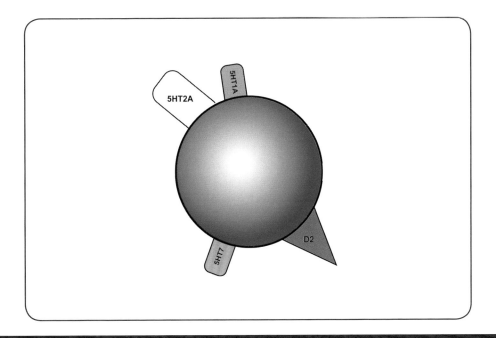

FIGURE 3.2. Lurasidone is a serotonin-dopamine antagonist in late stage clinical testing. This compound exhibits high affinity for both 5HT7 and 5HT1A receptors, and these serotonergic properties may explain some of lurasidone's clinical actions. Lurasidone also has minimal affinity for alpha 1 and alpha 2A adrenergic receptors, dopamine D1 and D3 receptors, and serotonin 5HT2C receptors. Interestingly, lurasidone lacks affinity for both H1 histamine and M1 cholinergic receptors, which enables the start of treatment at the therapeutically effective dose, allowing for a rapid onset of efficacy. Preliminary studies have shown that a dose of 80 mg/day is an effective treatment for acute exacerbation of schizophrenia. Doses of 40–120 mg/day have proven effective in clinical trials, and lurasidone appears to have a benign metabolic profile without affecting QTc prolongation. According to early results of clinical trials, once a day administration is possible and results in low risk of EPS, akathisia, metabolic effects, or weight gain. Lurasidone is currently in phase III clinical trials for the treatment of acute and chronic schizophrenia, as well as monotherapy and adjunctive treatment of bipolar depression. Actions at 5HT7 and 5HT1A receptors suggest potential antidepressant and pro-cognitive actions, but this requires confirmation in clinical trials and real world clinical experience.

Table 3.1.
The Future of Antipsychotics

Compounds	Properties and Notes
Glycine agonists	In addition to glutamate, glycine is necessary for the opening of NMDA receptors. Glycine, d-serine, or its analogue, d-cyclosporine, bind to the glycine site of the NMDA receptor and could potentially stimulate the NMDA receptors enough to overcompensate for their hypothetical hypofunction. Several glycine agonists are currently in clinical trials, and preliminary data suggest efficacy in treating positive, negative, and cognitive symptoms of schizophrenia.
GlyT1 inhibitors	Glycine transporter (GlyT1) inhibitors such as sarcosine block reuptake of glycine, thus increasing its synaptic availability; this could then lead to enhancement of NMDA neurotransmission and reversal of the hypofunctioning of NMDA receptors.
mGluR agents	mGluR2/3 are glutamate autoreceptors that provide negative feedback to the presynaptic neuron. Presynaptic receptor agonists could potentially decrease glutamate release in cortical areas. Preliminary data from early clinical trials suggest that mGluR agonists may be effective for treating both positive and negative symptoms of schizophrenia with low risk of metabolic or extrapyramidal side effects.
D3 partial agonists	D3 antagonists or partial agonists have a much higher binding affinity for D3 than D1 and D2 receptors. D3 receptors are located outside the synapse, where they are important for the tonic signaling in limbic areas of the brain. Dysfunction in D3 tonic firing has been hypothesized to underlie affective and negative symptoms in schizophrenia. Pharmaceutical agents that act on D3 receptors could potentially be useful in treating negative and cognitive symptoms, and preliminary data suggest they have a decreased risk of metabolic side effects associated with them.

Pharmaceutical Manipulation of Glutamate Neurotransmission

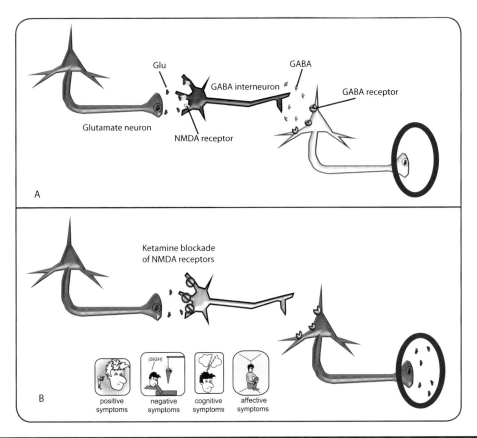

FIGURE 3.3. (A) Normal cortical glutamate regulation involves glutamate stimulation of NMDA receptors on GABA interneurons, leading to inhibition of glutamate (Glu) release. (B) In the phencyclidine (PCP)-ketamine model of schizophrenia, blockade of NMDA receptors results in disinhibition of glutamate neurons, leading to excessive Glu release. The fact that PCP induces schizophrenia-like symptoms has led to the NMDA hypofunction hypothesis of schizophrenia. Several of the novel medications currently being investigated are based on this theory: mGluR agonists can act on autoreceptors located on the presynaptic neuron to prevent excessive Glu release through a negative feedback mechanism; both glycine reuptake inhibitors and glycine agonists increase the amount of glycine present in the synapse leading to increased glutamate transmission, enhanced GABA release, and therefore greater downstream glutamate inhibition.

4

Optimizing Functional Outcomes in Schizophrenia

Chapter 4 aims to develop an understanding of the best treatment practices and maintenance methods for optimizing individual patient outcomes in schizophrenia. Determining the best treatment approach for patients with schizophrenia can be challenging. Different "pharmacies" that can be useful in the search for an effective treatment plan are presented in this chapter. Practical switching strategies that will aid in proper medication changes, when necessary, are also presented. Special consideration is given to the recent discussion regarding the importance of cognitive dysfunction in treatment outcomes.

Treating Positive and Negative Symptoms of Schizophrenia

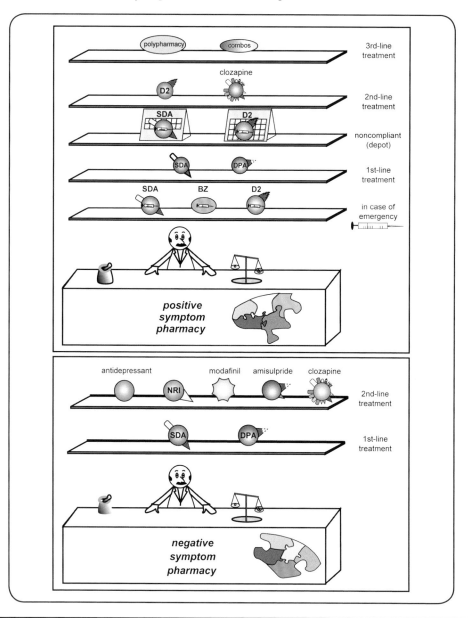

FIGURE 4.1. The best treatment for the positive and negative symptoms of schizophrenia.

Treating Metabolic Issues and Sedation

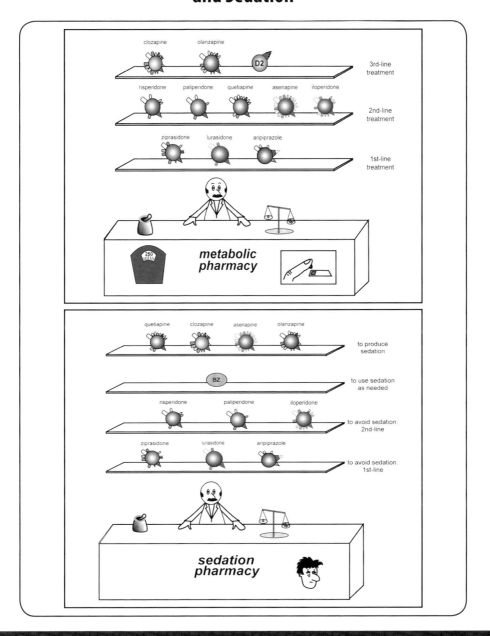

FIGURE 4.2. The best practices to avoid metabolic side effects and manage sedation in the treatment of schizophrenia.

Reducing Side Effects to Optimize Functional Outcome

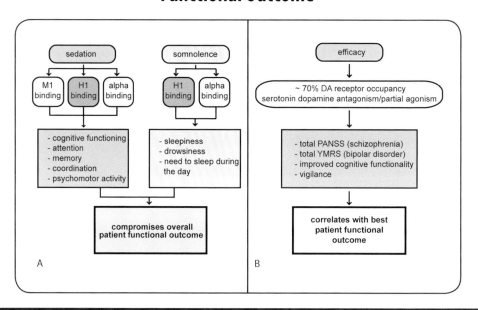

FIGURE 4.3. Several studies indicate that unacceptable side effects from treatment with antipsychotics can adversely affect functional outcome. (A) Blockade of dopamine D2, muscarinic M1, histamine H1, and/or alpha1 adrenergic receptors can lead to sedation, which can impact cognitive functioning, attention, memory, and coordination. All of these will result in poor overall functioning in patients with schizophrenia. Somnolence, which can lead to sleepiness and drowsiness, is most likely mediated by blockade of H1 and alpha1 adrenergic receptors. These symptoms can also affect the overall functioning of the patient. (B) An adequate treatment of schizophrenia aims to resolve positive symptoms as well as affective, cognitive, and negative symptoms. Pharmacologically, this requires approximately 70% blockade of D2 receptors in the nucleus accumbens in addition to antagonism/partial agonism of D2, 5HT2A, and 5HT1A receptors in other key brain regions. Antagonism of histamine H1, muscarinic M1, and alpha 1 adrenergic receptors is best avoided, as these lead to most of the side effects seen with antipsychotics.

Table 4.1.
Dosing and Side Effect Factors That May Affect Adherence

Medication non-adherence has been linked to poor functional outcome in schizophrenia. Several factors including adverse side effects and dosing schedule may affect patient adherence to a particular antipsychotic. In addition to long-acting depot formulations of conventional antipsychotics, several atypical antipsychotics are also available in long-acting depot formulations that may be especially useful for treating individuals with a history of medication non-adherence.

Atypical Antipsychotic	Dosing Schedule of Oral Formulation	Alternative Formulations		Side Effects*			Additional Caveats
		Long-Acting Depot	Other	Sedating	Weight Gain	EPS	
Aripiprazole	1X day	4 wk in trials	10 and 15 mg oral disintegrating tablets; 9.75 mg/1.3 injection	unusual	unusual	not unusual (can cause akathisia)	May be activating rather than sedating
Asenapine	2X day		Only available in 5 and 10 mg sublingual tablets	common	common	common	Patient should not eat or drink immediately after drug administration
Iloperidone	2X day	4 wk in trials		not unusual	not unusual	not unusual	Very gradual titration
Olanzapine	1X day	Approved but not available in the US 2 wk 4 wk	Oral disintegrating tablet	common	problematic	unusual	No titration needed. Oral supplementation of depot may be needed
Paliperidone	1X day	4 wk 12 wk in trials	Only available in extended release formulation	common	common	common	No titration needed
Quetiapine	1X day		Extended release formulation available	problematic	common	unusual	
Risperidone	1X day	2 wk 4 wk in early trials	0.5, 1, and 2 mg oral disintegrating tablets; 1 mg/mL liquid	common	common	common (dose-dependent)	Titration needed
Ziprasidone	2X day		10-20 mg IM formulation available	not unusual	common	not unusual	

*Side effects scale: Unusual = reported in few patients; Not unusual = occurs in a significant minority; Common = many experience or can be in significant amount; Problematic = occurs frequently, can be in a significant amount, and may be a health problem in some patients

Cognitive Dysfunction and Functional Outcome

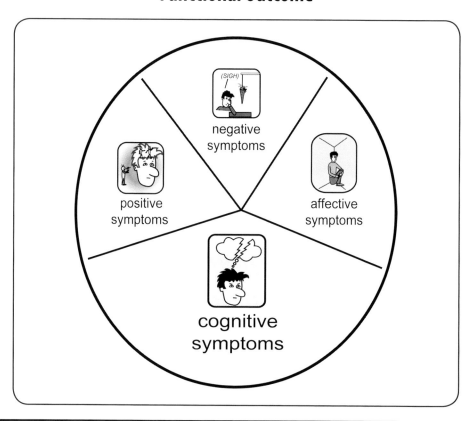

FIGURE 4.4. Recent data indicate that cognitive dysfunction is a better predictor of functional outcome than any other symptom domain. Although the importance of cognitive deficits to treatment outcome is recognized and accepted, cognitive impairment is not currently included in the diagnostic criteria for schizophrenia. Despite this fact, there is presently much discussion in the field as to the most effective ways to assess and treat cognitive deficits in schizophrenia. The Measurement and Treatment Research to Improve Cognition in Schizophrenia (MATRICS) initiative and the Cognitive Neuroscience Treatment to Improve Cognition in Schizophrenia (CNTRICS) initiative have sought to develop testing batteries that will allow for the assessment of cognitive dysfunction and its response to treatment options. It is likely that the development of treatments that can more adequately address the cognitive symptoms of schizophrenia will greatly enhance the ability of patients to function in society and lead fulfilling lives.

Switching Strategies:
Part 1

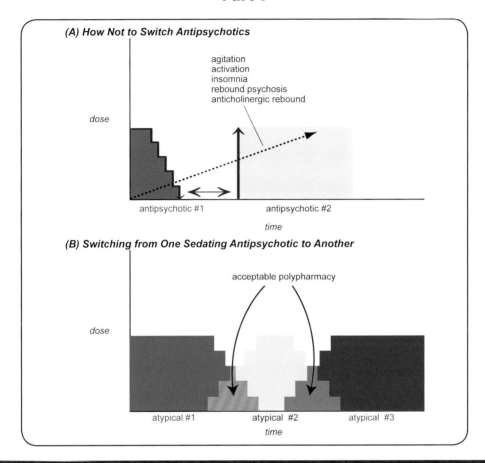

FIGURE 4.5. (A) There are strategies for switching antipsychotics and strategies to avoid in order to prevent rebound psychosis, aggravation of side effects, or withdrawal symptoms. Generally, it is preferable to (1) not rush the discontinuation of the first antipsychotic, (2) not allow gaps between two antipsychotic treatments, and (3) not start the second antipsychotic at full dose.

(B) Cross-titration is usually advised when switching from one sedating antipsychotic to another. As the first antipsychotic is slowly tapered off, the second antipsychotic is slowly added on. This can be done over a few days or weeks. Even though the patient will be simultaneously taking two medications for a short period of time, this is acceptable, as it can decrease side effects and the risk of rebound symptoms, and it can hasten the successful transition to the second drug.

Switching Strategies:
Part 2

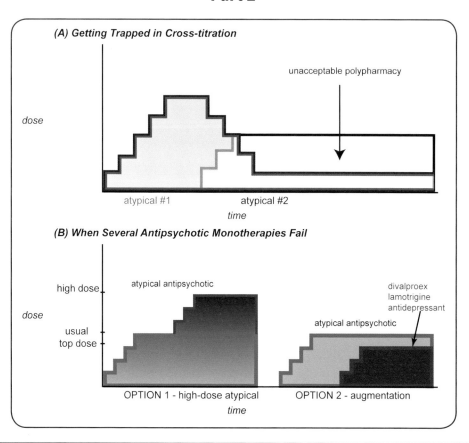

FIGURE 4.6. (A) When initiating cross-titration, it is imperative to not forget to taper the first drug. Patients may improve in the middle of a cross-titration, but this should not be a reason to stop the process. An unfinished cross-titration will lead to polypharmacy, in which the patient takes two drugs indefinitely. Although polypharmacy is sometimes a necessity in hard-to-treat cases, an adequate monotherapy trial of a second drug should be the first option.

(B) When a monotherapy with an atypical antipsychotic fails, the psychopharmacologist has few options. Left: A high dose of the atypical antipsychotic can be used; however, at high doses, some side effects that are not normally related to atypical antipsychotics may appear. Right: Augmentation with a mood stabilizer such as divalproex or lamotrigine or with an antidepressant could transform a previously ineffective atypical antipsychotic monotherapy into an efficacious drug cocktail.

Switching Strategies:
Part 3

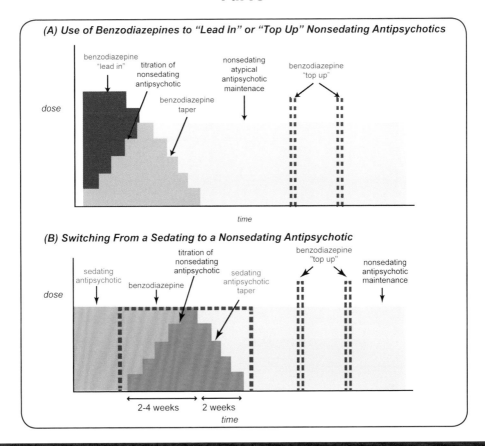

FIGURE 4.7. (A) Benzodiazepines (BZ) can be used to "lead in" or "top up" a nonsedating antipsychotic. For agitated patients, it may be beneficial to shortly augment with a BZ and use it as a "lead in" while initiating a nonsedating antipsychotic. Once the nonsedating antipsychotic has been titrated to its full dose, the BZ can be slowly tapered. During the maintenance phase of the antipsychotic, it can be helpful to use a BZ as a "top up" when needed by the patient.

(B) Switching from a sedating to a nonsedating antipsychotic can be problematic. One method to do so suggests adding a BZ before the nonsedating antipsychotic is titrated to its optimal therapeutic dose, while the sedating antipsychotic is still given at full dose. Once the sedating antipsychotic is slowly tapered and the patient is stable, the BZ can be stopped. "Topping up" can be used sporadically if agitation or insomnia occurs. This switching strategy may be best for patients who are switching because of inadequate symptom control by their sedating antipsychotic.

Switching Strategies:
Part 4

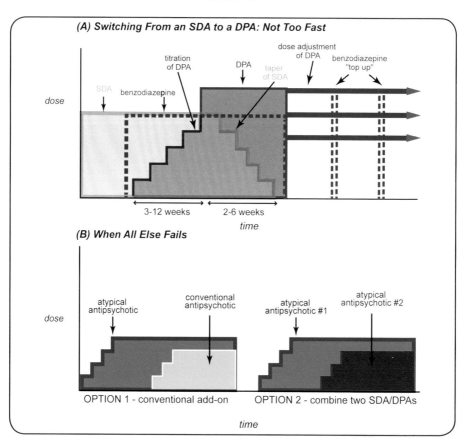

(A) Switching From an SDA to a DPA: Not Too Fast

(B) When All Else Fails

OPTION 1 - conventional add-on   OPTION 2 - combine two SDA/DPAs

FIGURE 4.8. (A) The emergence of psychosis, agitation, or insomnia can potentially hinder the switch from a 5HT2A/D2 antagonist (SDA) to a D2 partial agonist (DPA). The second antipsychotic can be gradually added while keeping the first one at full dose. Adding a benzodiazepine in the short term may be beneficial. After a few weeks, the SDA can be tapered and the benzodiazepine stopped. When switching to a DPA, it is important to give the receptors time to adjust their sensitivity; thus, the dose of the DPA may need to be adjusted in order to reach full therapeutic potential.

(B) When pushing the dose of an atypical antipsychotic or augmenting it with other drugs still fail, it might be necessary to combine two antipsychotics. A conventional antipsychotic (left) or an atypical antipsychotic such as an SDA or DPA (right) can be added to the first atypical drug. Although antipsychotic polypharmacy is frequently practiced, it has not been well studied and should only be used when every other approach has failed.

Summary

❖ The neurobiology underlying schizophrenia is complex and not completely understood; however, several neurotransmitter systems, including dopamine, serotonin, acetylcholine, and glutamate, are believed to be involved.

❖ Dopamine hyperfunction in the mesolimbic pathway is thought to be related to the positive symptoms (e.g., delusions) of schizophrenia. Hypofunction in the mesocortical dopamine pathway is thought to be involved in the negative (e.g., depression), cognitive, and affective symptoms.

❖ Conventional antipsychotics focus solely on lowering dopamine levels. Although these agents are often effective at reducing the positive symptoms, they do not treat the other symptom domains and have a high risk of adverse motor side effects associated with them.

❖ Atypical antipsychotics act on various receptors in addition to having effects at dopamine receptors. This molecular polypharmacy potentially allows for treatment of symptom domains other than the positive symptoms and avoids some of the motor side effects associated with conventional antipsychotics. However, atypical antipsychotics commonly have their own set of adverse side effects associated with them, including weight gain and sedation.

❖ Inadequate treatment of all symptom domains lessens the chance of successful functional outcome. Specifically, recent data highlight the association between cognitive dysfunction and poor functional outcome and suggest that successful treatment of schizophrenia must go beyond allaying only the positive symptoms.

❖ Numerous antipsychotics are currently available, each with a unique set of functional groups. These various receptor profiles provide the educated psychopharmacologist with a wealth of options for providing the most effective individual treatment course with the least adverse side effects.

❖ When determining the best treatment for an individual with schizophrenia, it may be necessary to try several different treatment strategies. Switching from one antipsychotic to another or employing polypharmacy must be done carefully to avoid problems.

❖ Several new agents are under investigation for their unique mechanisms of action. These drugs may prove more successful than the currently available antipsychotics in treating all the symptom domains of schizophrenia, thus leading to improved functional outcomes.

Suggested Reading

Agid O, Kapur S, and Remington G. Emerging drugs for schizophrenia. Expert Opin Emerging Drugs 2008;13(3):479–95.

Barnett JH, Robbins TW, Leeson VC et al. Assessing cognitive function in clinical trials of schizophrenia. Neurosci Biobehav Rev 2010 Jan 25. [Epub ahead of print]

Carter CS, Barch DM. Cognitive neuroscience-based approaches to measuring and improving treatment effects on cognition in schizophrenia: the CNTRICS initiative. Schizophr Bull 2007;33(5):1131-7.

Conn PJ, Lindsley CW, Jones CK. Activation of metabotropic glutamate receptors as a novel approach for the treatment of schizophrenia. Trends Pharmacol Sci 2009;30(1):25–31.

Emsley R. Drugs in development for the treatment of schizophrenia. Expert Opin Investig Drugs 2009;128(8):1103–18.

Ereshefsky L and Mascarenas CA. Comparison of the effects of different routes of antipsychotic administration on pharmacokinetics and pharmacodynamics. J Clin Psychiatry 2003;64(suppl 16):18-23.

Harvey PD, Howanitz E, Parrella M et al. Symptoms, cognitive functioning, and adaptive skills in geriatric patients with lifelong schizophrenia: a comparison across treatment sites. Am J Psychiatry 1998;155:1080–6.

Keefe RS, Silva SG, Perkins DO, Lieberman JA. The effects of atypical antipsychotic drugs on neurocognitive impairment in schizophrenia: a review and meta-analysis. Schizophr Bull 1999;25:201-22.

Kreyenbuhl J, Buchanan RW, Dickerson FB, Dixon LB. The schizophrenia patient outcomes research team (PORT): updated treatment recommendations 2009. Schizophr Bull 2010;36(1):94-103.

Kurtz MM, Wexler BE, Fujimoto M, Shagan DS, Seltzer JC. Symptoms versus neurocognition as predictors of change in life skills in schizophrenia after outpatient rehabilitation. Schizophr Res 2008;102:303-11.

Lipkovich IA, Deberdt W, Cseransky JG et al. Defining "good" and "poor" outcomes in patients with schizophrenia or schizoaffective disorder: a multidimensional data-driven approach. Psychiatry Res 2009;170:161-7.

McCann TV, Clark E, Lu S. Subjective side effects of antipsychotics and medication adherence in people with schizophrenia. J Advanced Nursing 2008;65(3):534-43.

Meyer JM, Loebel AD, and Scweizer E. Lurasidone: a new drug in development for schizophrenia. Expert Opin Investig Drugs 2009; 18(11):1715-26.

Novick D, Haro JM, Suarez D et al. Predictors and clinical consequences of non-adherence with antipsychotic medication in the outpatient treatment of schizophrenia. Psychiatry Res 2010;16:109-13.

Patel MX, David AS. Why aren't depot antipsychotics prescribed more often and what can be done about it? Advances in Psychiatric Treatment 2005;11:203-13.

Patil ST, Zhang L, Martenyi F et al. Activation of mGlu2/3 receptors as a new approach to treat schizophrenia; a randomized phase 2 clinical trial. Nat Medicine 2007;13(9):1102–7

Remington G, Foussias G, Agid O. Progress in defining optimal treatment outcome in schizophrenia. CNS Drugs 2010;24(1):9-20.

Seeman P and Guan H-C. Glutamate agonists for treating schizophrenia have high affinity for dopamine D2 and D3 receptors. Synapse 2009;63:705–9.

Sodhi M, Wood KH, Meador-Woodruff J. Role of glutamate in schizophrenia; integrating excitatory avenues of research. Expert Rev Neurother 2008;8(9):1389–1406.

Sokoloff P, Diaz J, De Foll B. The dopamine D3 receptor: a therapeutic target for the treatment of neuropsychiatric disorders. CNS Neurological Disorders - Drug Targets. 2006;5:25–43.

Stahl SM. Stahl's essential psychopharmacology. 3rd ed. New York: Cambridge University Press; 2008.

Stahl SM. Stahl's essential psychopharmacology: the prescriber's guide. 4th ed. New York: Cambridge University Press; in press.

CME Posttest

To receive your certificate of CME credit or participation, please complete the posttest (you must score at least 70% to receive credit) and activity evaluation answer sheet found on the last page and return it by mail or fax it to 760-931-8713. Once received, your posttest will be graded and, along with your certificate (if a score of 70% or more was attained), returned to you by mail. Alternatively, you may complete these items online and immediately print your certificate at **www.neiglobal.com/cme**. There is no fee for CME credits for this activity.

Please circle the correct answer on the answer sheet provided.

1. The positive symptoms of schizophrenia are hypothesized to result from:

     A. Mesocortical dopamine hypoactivity
     B. Mesocortical dopamine hyperactivity
     C. Mesolimbic dopamine hypoactivity
     D. Mesolimbic dopamine hyperactivity

2. According to the NMDA receptor hypofunction hypothesis of schizophrenia, glutamate hypofunction leads to:

     A. Mesocortical dopamine hypoactivity
     B. Mesolimbic dopamine hyperactivity
     C. All of the above
     D. None of the above

3. Stimulation of serotonin 5HT1A receptors:

     A. Leads to increased dopamine release and decreased glutamate release
     B. Leads to decreased dopamine release and decreased glutamate release
     C. Leads to decreased dopamine release and increased glutamate release
     D. Leads to increased dopamine release and increased glutamate release

4. Extrapyramidal side effects from conventional antipsychotics are believed to be a result of:

     A. D2 antagonism in the mesolimbic dopamine pathway
     B. D2 antagonism in the nigrostriatal dopamine pathway
     C. D2 antagonism in the tuberoinfundibular dopamine pathway
     D. D2 antagonism in the mesocortical dopamine pathway

5. In schizophrenia, functional outcome can be optimized by effectively treating:

     A. Positive symptoms
     B. Negative symptoms
     C. Cognitive symptoms
     D. All of the above

6. An inverse agonist leads to:

   A. Maximal signal transduction
   B. A level of signal transduction between that of an antagonist and a full agonist
   C. Less signal transduction than the absence of an agonist
   D. Greater signal transduction than that of a full agonist

7. A patient with schizophrenia presents with excessive weight and is otherwise at increased risk of developing cardiometabolic issues. Antipsychotics with which functional groups should be avoided to prevent further weight gain in this patient?

   A. Dopamine D2
   B. Serotonin 5HT2C and histamine H1
   C. Adrenergic alpha 1
   D. Muscarinic M1

8. Which atypical antipsychotic is available only as a sublingual formulation?

   A. Aripiprazole
   B. Ziprasidone
   C. Asenapine
   D. Lurasidone

9. Which of the following antipsychotics is not currently approved as a long-acting depot formulation?

   A. Quetiapine
   B. Risperidone
   C. Olanzapine
   D. Paliperidone

10. The novel atypical antipsychotic cariprazine that is currently under investigation is unique due to its:

   A. 5HT7 antagonism
   B. Glycine reuptake inhibitor actions
   C. D3 partial agonism that is stronger than its D2 affinity
   D. Metabotropic glutamate receptor agonism

Psychosis and Schizophrenia: Thinking It Through
Posttest and Activity Evaluation Answer Sheet

Please complete the posttest and activity evaluation answer sheet on this page and return by mail or fax. Alternatively, you may **complete these items online and immediately print your certificate at www.neiglobal.com/cme.**

Please circle the correct answer.

Posttest Answer Sheet (score of 70% or higher required for CME credit)

1.	A B C D	6.	A B C D
2.	A B C D	7.	A B C D
3.	A B C D	8.	A B C D
4.	A B C D	9.	A B C D
5.	A B C D	10.	A B C D

Activity Evaluation: Please rate the following, using a scale of:

1-poor　　**2-below average**　　**3-average**　　**4-above average**　　**5-excellent**

1. The overall quality of the <u>content</u> was…　　　　　　　　　　　1 2 3 4 5

2. The overall quality of this <u>activity</u> was…　　　　　　　　　　1 2 3 4 5

3. The relevance of the content to my professional needs was…　　　1 2 3 4 5

4. The level at which the learning objective was met of teaching me to understand the importance of cognitive factors in schizophrenia, including evolving new diagnostic criteria and methods for assessing cognition in clinical practice:　　　　　　　　　　　　　　　　　1 2 3 4 5

5. The level at which the learning objective was met of teaching me to differentiate antipsychotic drug treatments from each other on the basis of pharmacologic mechanisms and evidence-based clinical trial results:　　1 2 3 4 5

6. The level at which the learning objective was met of teaching me to develop treatment strategies that are designed to enhance adherence:　　1 2 3 4 5

7. The level at which the learning objective was met of teaching me to combine practical experience with evolving new evidence in order to integrate new and soon-to-be introduced treatments into clinical practice:　　1 2 3 4 5

8. The level at which this activity was objective, scientifically balanced, and free of commercial bias was…　　　　　　　　　　　　1 2 3 4 5

9. Based on my experience and knowledge, the level of this activity was…

　　　　　　Too Basic　　Basic　　Appropriate　　Complex　　Too Complex

10. My confidence level in understanding and treating this topic has _____ as a result of participation in this activity.

    A. Increased
    B. Stayed the same
    C. Decreased

11. Based on the information presented in this activity, I will…

    L. Change my practice
    M. Seek additional information on this topic
    N. Do nothing as current practice reflects activity's recommendations
    O. Do nothing as the content was not convincing

12. What barriers might keep you from implementing changes in your practice you'd like to make as a result of participating in this activity?

13. The following additional information about this topic would help me in my practice:

14. How could this activity have been improved?

15. Number of credits I am claiming, commensurate with the extent of my participation in the activity (maximum of 3.0): _____

Name (print): _____ Credentials: _____

Address: _____

_____

City: _____ State: _____ Zip Code: _____

Phone: _____ Fax: _____

Email: _____

I certify that I completed this CME activity (signature): _____
                                                                                Date

Mail or fax **both sides** of this form to:

Mail: CME Department
           Neuroscience Education Institute
           1930 Palomar Point Way, Suite 101
           Carlsbad, CA 92008

Fax: (760) 931-8713
Attn: CME Department